Competing for a Sustainable World
Building Capacity for Sustainable Innovation

COMPETING
FOR A
SUSTAINABLE
WORLD

BUILDING
CAPACITY
FOR
SUSTAINABLE
INNOVATION

Sanjay Sharma

Greenleaf
PUBLISHING

© 2014 Greenleaf Publishing Limited

Published by Greenleaf Publishing Limited
Aizlewood's Mill
Nursery Street
Sheffield S3 8GG
UK
www.greenleaf-publishing.com

Cover by LaliAbril.com

Printed in the UK on environmentally friendly, acid-free paper
from managed forests by CPI Group (UK) Ltd, Croydon

British Library Cataloguing in Publication Data:
  A catalogue record for this book is available from the British Library.

  ISBN-13: 978-1-78353-224-7 [hardback]
  ISBN-13: 978-1-78353-122-6 [paperback]
  ISBN-13: 978-1-78353-123-3 [PDF ebook]
  ISBN-13: 978-1-78353-142-4 [ePub ebook]

Contents

Foreword

Stuart L. Hart

It has been nearly 20 years since I first wrote an article that ultimately appeared in the *Harvard Business Review* entitled "Beyond Greening: Strategies for a Sustainable World." The article stressed that corporate "greening" strategies aimed at incrementally reducing negative social and environmental impacts, while important, would not be nearly adequate to the challenge of global sustainability in the decades ahead. Even then, it was clear that "beyond greening" strategies—leapfrog clean technologies, and business models that included and lifted the 4+ billion poor in the developing world—would be essential if we were to fundamentally change the course of the global economy, and set it on a course to sustainability.

Now, nearly two decades later, I write with some good news and some bad news. First the good news: More and more corporations and entrepreneurs have begun to experiment with "beyond greening" strategies. Indeed, "clean technology" has become a fashionable investment category and "base of the pyramid" business models have become *de rigueur.* My own book, *Capitalism at the Crossroads,* which first appeared in 2005, was focused on building the content and business case for these strategies. But now for the bad news: Most "beyond greening" strategies are structured either as separate (external) investments, or are relegated to the corporate foundation or philanthropic arm of the company and framed as part of firms' corporate social responsibility (CSR) obligation.

In other words, despite progress on the strategy content front, we have made little headway in embedding or internalizing sustainable innovation into the organizational DNA of corporations. The result is that few of these strategic initiatives have scaled or achieved the kind of transformative change that is needed. A few corporations and entrepreneurs have begun to heed this call. Most, however, come from the emerging markets of Asia, India, and Latin America: Think Tata, ITC, Himin Solar, and Natura. Most large incumbents from the U.S., Western Europe, and Japan have yet to seriously confront this challenge.

The simple reality is that current corporate organizational structures are designed for self-replication—producing more of the same or, at best, continuously improving/adapting current products and processes. Yet growing social inequality and environmental degradation steadily render self-replication and continuous improvement obsolete. Not surprisingly, sustainable innovation calls for a fundamentally different set of organizational structures, systems, processes, and mindsets; since the existing corporate "immune system" is very strong, any project that deviates too far from the norm is quickly surrounded by "antibodies" and rendered harmless!

It is for the above reasons that Sanjay Sharma's book is so important and could not come at a more important time. In this book, Professor Sharma directly confronts and addresses the cognitive, psychological, and organizational challenges of global sustainability for corporations. Building a sustainable organization, he observes, "requires a firm to … fundamentally change its strategy in order to deliver both short-term and long-term economic, social, and environmental performance as per expectations of its various stakeholders (including its investors and shareholders)." Developing an effective strategy to generate successful sustainable innovations thus challenges firms to: (1) Build the business logic for sustainability; (2) Build managerial motivations; and (3) Build critical capabilities and skills. Sharma deftly integrates and extends existing work on Stakeholder Assessment, Opportunity Framing, and Capability Building and offers new and important guidance to firms on how to effectively develop and implement sustainable business strategies.

This book summarizes a lifetime of experience by the author that others in this emerging field—academics and practitioners alike—will find very useful and important. Sanjay has been a close personal friend and colleague for most of the past two decades. He rapidly ascended the academic ladder, becoming a prestigious Canada Research Chair, before becoming Dean of the John Molson School of Business at Concordia University in Montreal, and now the University of Vermont. But few people realize that, before his career as a successful academic (and now Dean), he had more than 15 years of corporate experience, working in India, Asia, and Africa. He therefore brings a unique perspective, combining practical corporate experience, with the mind of a scholar and, now, senior University executive.

Perhaps most importantly, Sanjay Sharma aims to practice what he preaches. He is in the midst of applying the thinking in this book directly in his role as Dean of the Business School at the University of Vermont. He is spearheading the transformation of the school by making sustainability the centerpiece of its strategy. Indeed, a completely new Sustainable Entrepreneurship MBA Program (SEMBA) is being developed and launched applying many of the principles articulated in this book. And I am honored to be joining the faculty at the University of Vermont to help in the exciting (and path-breaking) process of Building the Capacity for Sustainable Innovation at a U.S. business school. Our aim is nothing less than to transform the concept of business education to meet the challenges of the 21st century. Stay tuned.

Stuart L. Hart
Grossman Endowed Chair in Sustainable Business
University of Vermont

Preface

The journey

This book has been almost fifteen years in the making. In the late 1990s when I started teaching a course titled "Competitive Strategy for a Sustainable World" for MBA and executive audiences, I could not find a book that captured the state of the knowledge about the field of sustainable business. There were many books with interesting case studies but none that clearly laid out the steps or the process which firms could follow in order to transform themselves and compete successfully with sustainable business models, products, and services. I was often asked by students and publishers to write a book that could be used as a text for such courses and executive modules. As everyone who has undertaken to write a book knows, it is a time-consuming task that requires the author to put other pursuits on hold. I was at a stage in my career where my focus was on conceptual and empirical research studies to create new knowledge that could be disseminated through high-impact academic journals. These studies were critical at that stage of evolution of the field because we knew little about how organizations could compete successfully in a society that was increasingly concerned about environmental preservation and social justice. Of course, several thoughtful and important books were also published around this period to inform both organizations and researchers.

In 2005, Stuart Hart published *Capitalism at the Crossroads: The Unlimited Business Opportunities in Solving the World's Most Difficult Problems*. This book solved an immediate pedagogical need for me because this book expressed many of the ideas that were central to my philosophy. I now had a book that could form the core of my course and I could continue to add a few articles and cases from different perspectives. The reason the book resonated so well with my students and with me was because Stuart Hart's academic work has influenced my own research and thinking. We have collaborated since 1998 on research, teaching, executive education, and consulting in an attempt to practice what we preach. Chapter 7 on competing in the base of the pyramid is based in major part on our joint work published in 2004 in the *Academy of Management Executive*. Some of these ideas were developed while I was a Fulbright Fellow at the Kenan-Flagler Business School at UNC-Chapel Hill in 2001 and also appear in Hart's *Capitalism at the Crossroads*.

I would like to acknowledge others who contributed to my evolution as a sustainability scholar, educator, and consultant. My dissertation adviser at the University of Calgary and co-author Harrie Vredenburg and co-author Amy Pablo were mentors at an early stage of my academic career. I have had a productive professional partnership with Mark Starik since 2001 and we have co-edited several books. Another long-lasting professional collaborator partner is Alberto Aragon-Correa with whom I have published several academic articles and co-edited a book. Alberto and I also co-founded a scholarly society called the Group of Researchers on Organizations and the Environment (GRONEN). In 2001, we discussed the need for a small research-focused meeting that would be held every other year in Europe and would bring together scholars from North America and Europe. GRONEN has lasted longer than I (and perhaps Alberto) expected: after bi-annual meetings in Granada, St. Gallen, Cyprus,

Milan, and Provence, the 2014 meeting will be in Helsinki. The 2016 meeting is already being planned. Ongoing conversations, collaborations, and friendships with many scholars and practitioners of sustainability over the past four decades have influenced my thinking. For fear of omitting names, I will refrain from attempting to list all the wonderful scholars who have engaged in stimulating intellectual exchanges and have influenced my scholarship.

In addition to over twenty years in academia, I also came to this book after sixteen years as a manager in multinational enterprises on three continents. During this period spent in several developing and developed countries, I observed the complex social and environmental outcomes and impacts of routine managerial decisions. I realized that my business education had not prepared me to understand these complexities. As an academic, after being awarded a prestigious Canada Research Chair in Organizational Sustainability and setting up and running a Centre for Responsible Organizations at Wilfrid Laurier University, I began the next phase of my career as a Dean in order to help integrate sustainable business thinking in business school curricula and research.

As the Dean of the largest business school in Canada, the John Molson School of Business at Concordia University in Montreal, I began by changing the way that the school ran its operations, to bring in more sustainable practices. These included a new LEED-certified 400,000 square foot building with a unique solar wall. I also helped bring more courses on sustainability and funds for graduate students focused on business sustainability research. I conceived a center for sustainable enterprise that would foster research across business and non-business disciplines and disseminate this research to practitioners. Funded by a generous donation by David O'Brien, the Chairman of two Canadian companies (Encana and RBC), the David O'Brien Centre for Sustainable Enterprise became a reality. Paul Shrivastava became its first Director and has been instrumental in developing this center into a world-class nexus of research and practice. As Dean of the University of Vermont School of Business Administration, I led a process to revamp the undergraduate curriculum with sustainable business as one of the three cores (global business and entrepreneurship are the other two) and the MBA program around a theme of sustainable entrepreneurship focused on developing clean technology and sustainable business projects. Since 2011, I have been involved with Stuart Hart's initiatives in developing the Emergent Institute (formerly the Indian Institute of Sustainable Enterprise) in India and with his NGO, Enterprise for a Sustainable World.

During this period, over numerous conversations with managers in various organizations I came to the conclusion that there was need for a book that would describe and lay out systematically the steps that organizations could take in order to build a capacity to undertake a strategy that would enable them to compete in a world that was increasingly focused on addressing major sustainability challenges. Regardless of how political decisions and regulations evolve in different countries, business has to prepare itself to compete successfully for a future that is being determined by society rather than by governments and politicians.

This book is intended for a wide variety of audiences including academics, managers in corporations, not-for-profits, government agencies, educators, and general audiences interested in learning more about how business can be successful and contribute to a more sustainable world. Some of the ideas in this book are my own, some are developed collaboratively with other scholars, and some have been drawn from the remarkable work of the many scholars who have furthered the progress of the field of sustainable business. All errors are my own.

The role of business in a sustainable world

Many people are skeptical about whether or not business has a role in addressing the world's major sustainability challenges. I would argue that businesses constitute such a dominant portion of the global economy that solutions that exclude them are bound to fail unless almost all the countries in the world change their dominant political and economic systems. Sometime during the 2000s, inter-firm transfers of direct investments between countries became larger than the transfers of aid between governments from international financial institutions such as the IMF and the World Bank. The gap between the accelerating private flows of global fund transfers and the slowing aid from the developed world to the developing world is growing rapidly. This lends greater urgency to the need to ensure that these investments lead to projects with positive social and environmental impacts rather than developing traditional business models based on centuries-old technologies and systems that were created during the Industrial Revolution. Accelerating and scaling up traditional technologies and business models will further damage our fragile ecosystems and create greater social inequities that spawn increasing conflicts, terrorism, and wars. At the same time, as business attempts to engage the four billion people at the base of the income pyramid (BOP), there is real danger that such business models could create further irreversible environmental damage and social injustice. As the lower-income and unserved markets expand, adopting traditional business models may result in forever losing the opportunity and window of time to create new forms of business that generate positive social, environmental, and economic value simultaneously.

Sustainability challenges such as climate change and the loss of species diversity and ecosystems transcend national borders. Governments without the mandate to act beyond their own borders are powerless to address these great challenges. They seek to do so via international agreements such as the Kyoto Protocol or international regimes such as the United Nations Environment Program. However, as we know, writing twenty-three years after the Rio de Janeiro conference in 1991, these international agreements have not been effectively implemented and the international regimes do not have the mandate to require sovereign governments to take action. Civil society in the form of nongovernmental organizations (NGOs) continues to multiply to address the failure of governments. However,

NGOs generally have a localized operating domain and a focus on a single issue, for example, the decontamination of well water infused with arsenic in a region of Bangladesh. While NGOs play a critical role in addressing government and market failures at the micro level, they lack the resources to scale up their operations to have an impact on a national or global scale. Businesses have the resources, technology, global reach, and motivation to innovate in their self-interest to develop the basis for long-term future competitive advantage in a world that demands sustainable performance from its institutions. The self-interest of business lies in:

- Future growth and disruptive innovation opportunities at the base of the pyramid (BOP) markets that have four billion people with unmet needs

- The inexorable march toward destruction of ecosystems that is depleting the resources and degrading the environments on which businesses are dependent for free services

- Unpredictable weather patterns due to climate change that add considerable risk and cost to business operations and their supply chains; and

- The rising social inequities that spark more frequent political conflicts, terrorism, and instability that makes it difficult, risky, and expensive for business to operate

The conventional business models of the past several centuries are eroding. Under the conventional model, a business generated profits without consideration of unregulated negative environmental or social impacts as long as it complied with the prevalent laws. It paid its taxes and expected governments to manage its negative social and environmental impacts. It created charitable foundations separate from the core business through which it gave back to society via philanthropy. Society no longer accepts this separation. It expects business to address its negative social and environmental impacts while it creates shareholder value. At the same time, societal understanding of what constitutes a sustainable practice or outcome is rapidly evolving. Businesses have to evolve with, and participate in, this understanding and learn to adapt and change so that they can develop strategies to successfully compete in a world that demands that firms not only create shareholder value but also contribute to greater social justice and equity while preserving natural capital. This book is intended to help managers understand how they can develop business logic, change their organizations, change managerial mind-sets and decision-making, and build critical capabilities in order to compete in a sustainable world. At the same time, it is important to keep in mind that sustainability is a journey and not an end state that a firm can reach at a certain point in time. The race is on, and several firms have a head start on this journey. Hopefully, this book will help others catch up.

Charlotte, Vermont
2014

One
What is corporate sustainability?

All men have stars, but they are not the same things for different people. For some, who are travelers, the stars are guides. For others they are no more than little lights in the sky. For others, who are scholars, they are problems... But all these stars are silent.

Antoine de Saint-Exupéry, *writer, poet, philosopher, and aviator*

Sustainability has different meanings for different people. It has different meanings in different contexts. It has different meanings at different points of time: in the past, at present, and in the future. The meaning of sustainability is constantly evolving, sometimes slowly and sometimes in great leaps and bounds as new knowledge is created and scientific discoveries made. For example, knowledge about the impact of chemicals on human health, the depletion of the Earth's ozone layer, the impact of greenhouse gases on global warming, the thinning of the polar ice caps, global warming and rise in ocean levels, the impact of industrial pollution on air and water quality, habitats, and species, has evolved constantly over the last five decades.

In this book, sustainability refers to resilience and the longevity of our ecosystems (which includes minerals, vegetation, oceans, atmosphere, climate, water bodies, and biodiversity), society (which includes culture, languages, and quality of life) and economy. A sustainable world is one in which the human race enjoys a high quality of life in an equitable and just society and a thriving ecosystem that includes a biodiversity of plants and animals, and clean atmosphere/air, water, soils, and oceans. The concept of a sustainable world may sound utopian and perhaps impossible to achieve. However, it is difficult to argue that this is an ideal not worth striving for. If we reverse the argument, it would be difficult for a rational person to adopt a position that economic growth and prosperity is worthwhile at all costs including deteriorating air and water quality, growth of diseases and cancers, destruction of species, destruction of nature, decreased quality of life, and increasing social injustice and inequality. Ecosystems, society, and the economy are intertwined and interdependent. Businesses are embedded in, draw from, and affect society and the environment. While all sectors—governments, communities, consumers, civil society, and business—have a role to play in the journey toward the ideal of a sustainable world, this book is about the role of business.

Managers are exposed to, and sometimes bombarded with, multiple terms in the media with different meanings attributed to sustainability. Different consultants often use the terms differently. Some of the terms used include corporate social responsibility (CSR), corporate citizenship, greening, sustainable development, and corporate sustainability. The term in vogue may vary depending on the country or region. While all these terms refer to one or more aspects of a firm's strategy and actions intended to address its social and environmental impacts, there are some differences. Understanding these differences helps managers engage in meaningful dialogue with different stakeholders and constituents in order to define a problem domain, develop effective strategies, and generate successful sustainable innovations.

In Australia, New Zealand, and many Western European countries, CSR is used synonymously with corporate sustainability. In other contexts, CSR refers to a firm assuming responsibility for the impacts that society deems as negative or unacceptable, rather than fundamentally changing its strategy and operations to generate positive social and environmental impacts. The negative social and environmental impacts that a responsible firm needs to address are a moving target. This is because society's perspectives about which impacts of business's operations are negative are constantly evolving. For example, societal perceptions about emissions of waste from manufacturing facilities have changed substantially over the last five decades. Visual representations such as smokestacks represented economic development in the 1950s, but they now represent air pollution for most people across the world.

The term "corporate citizenship" is usually used to describe a firm's role in, or responsibility toward, society. In some contexts, it is used interchangeably with CSR and some companies use it to describe their social and community initiatives. Some firms emphasize the term "corporate philanthropy". Corporate philanthropy usually refers to corporate giving or donations intended to mitigate government failures in addressing social needs, problems, and challenges. Another term used in various contexts is corporate greening. Greening refers to actions adopted by firms to reduce negative impacts on the natural environment and usually does not focus on negative social impacts.

Regardless of how these terms are actually used by firms, or are defined by scholars, none of these—CSR, citizenship, or philanthropy—necessarily implies that the firm will change its core operations or strategies. Usually, these terms are used to describe a firm's practices and actions to mitigate the impacts of its operations that society deems negative. As compared to the terms discussed above, corporate sustainability as defined in this book has fundamental implications for business strategy. In this book *corporate sustainability refers to a firm's strategy that enables it to achieve positive economic, social, and environmental performance.* As highlighted above, it may not be possible for any organization to be truly and completely sustainable. Rather, corporate sustainability is a journey on which an increasing number of organizations have embarked.

The term "sustainable" is a derivation of the term "sustainable development" that was coined by the World Commission on Environment and Development (WCED). The WCED, more popularly known as the Brundtland Commission (after its Chair, Gro Harlem Brundtland) was created by the United Nations in 1983 to address growing concern about the accelerating deterioration of the human environment and natural resources and its consequences for economic and social development. In its report, *Our Common Future*, published in 1987, the WCED coined the most often-quoted definition of sustainable development as development that "meets the needs of the present without compromising the ability of future generations to meet their own needs."[1] This definition placed economic development within the context of resources (natural environment) and also within the context of balancing development in the present and in the future, and equity between societal groups and across generations.

The WCED definition called for businesses to adopt three principles of sustainability: sustainability of resource extraction—should not exceed the capacity of natural systems to regenerate resources such as forests, fisheries, soil, clean water, etc.; sustainability of waste generation—should not exceed the carrying capacity of natural systems to absorb them; and social equity—business activities should have a positive impact on poverty reduction, distribution of income, and human rights. Hence, this definition is relevant to corporate sustainability and the role of business in sustainable development, as defined in this book.

Karl-Henrik Robèrt, a Swedish oncologist, translated the WCED definition into system conditions for sustainability via the Natural Step Framework in 1989. These four conditions called for eliminating humanity's contribution to the progressive build-up of substances extracted from the Earth's crust; eliminating humanity's contribution to the progressive build-up of chemicals and compounds; eliminating humanity's contribution to the progressive physical degradation and destruction of nature and natural processes; and eliminating humanity's contribution to conditions that undermine people's capacity to meet their basic human needs.

These central elements of sustainable development as proposed by WCED and the Natural Step are fairly similar. However, they are relatively easy to visualize at a global, national or a societal level but are much more difficult for an individual firm to measure and implement. At the firm level, sustainability can be broadly translated into strategies that lead to *the achievement of its short-term financial, social, and environmental performance without compromising its long-term financial, social, and environmental performance*. This means that the firm needs to create value for its stakeholders in the present while investing in strategies and resources to improve the social, environmental, and economic performance desired by its stakeholders (including its shareholders) in the future. In this process, the firm has to manage the uncertainty related to the evolving and changing definition of "value" over time for its various stakeholders.

A sustainable organization is one that changes its business or its strategy to achieve not only its economic or core objectives (for example, for a nonprofit organization, the core objective may be the delivery of healthcare or clean water rather than profits), but also its social and environmental performance. Hence, a sustainable organization is significantly different from a firm that does not fundamentally change its business model or strategy but rather acts *responsibly* by adopting practices to mitigate the negative social and environmental impacts of its *existing* operations. How firms can undertake the journey to transform themselves into sustainable organizations is the focus of this book.

Building capacity for sustainable innovation

Building a sustainable organization requires a firm to analyze and fundamentally change its strategy in order to deliver both short-term and long-term economic, social, and environmental performance as per the expectations of its various stakeholders, including its investors and shareholders. An effective strategy to generate and implement successful sustainable innovations requires the firm to:

- Identify relevant and material sustainability issues
- Understand linkages between sustainable practices and competitive advantage
- Build business logic for a sustainable strategy
- Build managerial motivations
- Build critical capabilities

Identifying relevant and material sustainability issues requires the generation of data on the firm's sustainability impacts that need to be addressed by a strategic analysis of the firm's sustainability footprint. This includes measuring and benchmarking a firm's social and environmental footprint in addition to its economic metrics based on salience of issues that are important for the firm's stakeholders and estimating the impacts of these issues on current and future business (Chapter 2). Before developing a strategy, managers need to understand the risks of following an unsustainable strategy and the linkage between a sustainable strategy and competitive advantage (Chapter 3). Building logic requires an understanding of how sustainable value generates corporate value in terms of enhancing the core utilities for the customers served by the firm (Chapter 4). Building managerial motivations requires changing mind-sets and creating an opportunity frame to motivate employees to become change agents for a sustainable organization (Chapter 5). Building critical capabilities involves embedding unique processes within the firm to engage and integrate stakeholders, generate information and higher order learning, and generate continuous innovation of processes, products, services and business models that enhance triple bottom-line performance and enable the firm to compete in the future in existing markets (Chapter 6), and the co-creation of sustainable business models for the unserved and under-served four billion people at the base of the pyramid (Chapter 7). Figure 1.1 graphically depicts the building blocks of a sustainable organization. As the figure shows, the logic, motivations, and capabilities closely interact to produce sustainable innovations and these innovations in turn impact the logic, motivations, and capabilities. Finally, Chapter 9 offers a vision for the next steps forward in enabling businesses to leverage their resources on this journey toward a sustainable economy.

Figure 1.1 **The building blocks of a sustainable organization**

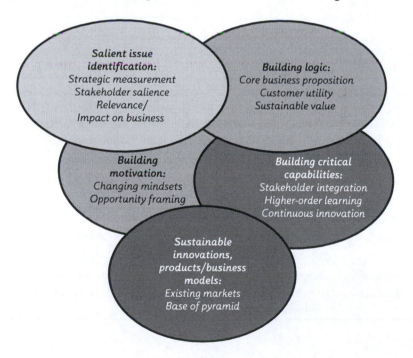

Summary

A sustainable organization develops core strategies and business models for the achievement of its short-term financial, social, and environmental goals without compromising its ability to compete in the future on its long-term financial, social, and environmental goals. This contrasts with concepts such as corporate social responsibility and corporate citizenship that emphasize investing in practices to mitigate or reduce the negative social and environmental impacts of the organization's existing operations. Table 1.1 highlights the differences among terms commonly used to refer to an organization's actions to address its social and environmental impacts.

Table 1.1 **Terms used within the domain of corporate sustainability**

Term	Description
Corporate social responsibility	Actions and/or practices that respond to societal concerns about negative social and environmental impacts of a firm's existing operations
Corporate citizenship	A firm's role in, and/or responsibility toward, society. Often the practices associated with citizenship include complying with the laws, engaging the community, and giving back to the community
Corporate philanthropy	Corporate giving or donations to address social needs, problems, and challenges
Corporate greening	Actions to reduce negative impacts on the natural environment—usually does not account for negative social impacts
Corporate sustainability	Fundamental changes in core strategies and operations to achieve positive economic, social, and environmental performance

Two
Identifying salient sustainability issues

> Wall Street is waking up to climate change risks and opportunities. Considerably more of the world's largest corporations are getting a handle on what climate change means for their business and what they need to do to capture opportunities and mitigate risks. This all points to a continued elevation of climate change as a critical shareholder value issue for investors.
>
> James Cameron, *Chairman of the Carbon Disclosure Project (CDP), September 2005*

Building a sustainable organization that can compete effectively on the triple bottom-line performance requires innovative strategy, processes, products/services, and business models. Such innovation is only possible with deep engagement and active involvement of the firm's managers and employees. Managers and employees can potentially bring past learning, experience, history, and deep insights into the operational issues within their jurisdiction, and offer innovative solutions to external challenges. However, the ability of managers to generate new ideas and innovations that lead to positive economic, social, and environmental impacts depends on an understanding of how the operations of their firm, and more specifically the operations that they are responsible for, not only impact the firm's profitability but also society and the natural environment. Managers need information and data on how much the operations under their jurisdiction contribute to carbon dioxide and other greenhouse gas emissions, ground level ozone, drinking water quality, biodiversity in the ecosystem that they operate in; and negative impacts on society such as reducing gainful employment, number of people earning below living wage, respiratory or other diseases affecting human health, increasing income equality, and reducing economic opportunities for current and future generations. Being able to see these impacts quantitatively and relative to other firms in the industry nationally and internationally enables the managers to make connections between their decisions and outcomes on economic, social, and environmental performance. Therefore, the sustainability footprint is not just about measuring the social and environmental impacts, but also about:

1. Benchmarking these impacts against other firms in the industry

2. Analyzing the relevance of these impacts for the firm based on the issues that are critical for the firm's salient stakeholders

3. Analyzing the relevance of these impacts on the firm's short-term and long-term economic performance

4. Assessing how the actions and decisions of managers can generate positive social, environmental, and economic impacts

Due to their unfamiliarity with actions required to meet the multiple sustainability challenges, most managers often feel overwhelmed in this unfamiliar terrain. They often feel that at best they can focus narrowly only on one aspect of their sustainability footprint, such as the firm's or a facility's carbon emissions. Therefore, they focus on measuring only a few social and environmental impact(s). However, a more comprehensive understanding of a firm's sustainability footprint is important for building a sustainable organization. Comprehensive information about the firm's sustainability footprint does not mean that it has to immediately develop a strategy to tackle all elements of this footprint. Rather, a complete picture of the footprint enables the managers to develop the best match between their capabilities and the innovations required for generating the positive and social and environmental impacts that simultaneously enable the firm to compete effectively in the short term and the long term. Ultimately, after looking at a comprehensive picture of its sustainability footprint, a firm may decide that its best strategy is to focus immediately on reducing its carbon footprint, but this decision should be taken after an analysis of the complete picture. This is because new opportunities and innovative business models may emerge at the interactions between various social, environmental, and economic impacts. By focusing too narrowly only on one element such as its carbon emissions, the firm may miss potential future opportunities for new innovations. For example, a power utility that decides to reduce its carbon footprint may focus on carbon capture and sequestration and miss business opportunities to develop innovative new distributed wind and solar technologies and business models that may position it for high growth in emerging markets and also enable it to offset its carbon emissions.

At the same time, environmental and social issues are frequently connected or enmeshed. For example, growing coffee has environmental impacts of habitat destruction. These can be addressed by growing coffee in the shade without clearing forests. Coffee farms also have social impacts in terms of fair prices paid to farmers and displacement of communities on lands that are forcibly acquired by powerful businesses and governments. Similarly, there are major environmental and social impacts of extracting minerals such as gold, cobalt, and tantalum for use in electronic devices such as mobile phones and tablets. These operations often finance wars, conflicts, and genocide in countries such as the Congo. Similarly, extraction of diamonds not only destroys habitats and poisons water bodies but also finances genocide and wars in several countries. The gathering of natural pearls leads to the destruction of coral reefs and exploitation of the pearl-gathering communities. Therefore, it is not often possible for a firm to focus only on one element of their footprint at a time but rather it needs to develop a holistic strategy to address multiple social and environmental impacts.

As firms begin to measure some of these impacts, they are surprised to learn not only the extent of the unseen and far-reaching social and environmental impacts that emanate from their operations, but also the opportunities that emerge connected to these impacts. Ray Anderson, the CEO of Interface, referred to this process as "climbing the sustainability mountain," indicating that with each insight and understanding of a negative and social impact, the real magnitude of the challenge facing the company grew. Within these challenges, potential business opportunities to address these challenges emerged for Interface,[2] the company that Anderson founded.

It is important to keep in mind that multiple stakeholders increasingly expect firms to improve their sustainability footprint along their entire value chain. Many customers and NGOs want firms to take responsibility for environmental and social impacts in their value chain. This includes a firm's suppliers, its suppliers' suppliers, and consumption and disposal of its products. In response, firms such as Wal-Mart are working on a sustainability index that surveys more than 100,000 global suppliers to evaluate their sustainability footprint. Wal-Mart wants to respond to stakeholder concerns by increasing transparency in its supply chain. Wal-Mart has also created a Sustainability Consortium to enable it to work with suppliers, retailers, nongovernmental organizations (NGOs), universities, and government officials to conduct research and develop data and tools that will enable research-driven product sustainability measurement and reporting. The intent of the consortium is to develop a global database of information on products' lifecycles, from raw materials to disposal. Measuring the impacts will enable Wal-Mart to improve the sustainability performance of the products it sells and help its vendors understand and improve their own sustainability performance. Wal-Mart would ultimately like to provide customers with information about products in a simple, easy-to-understand sustainability index.[3] Similarly, Procter & Gamble has been a pioneer in analyzing the life-cycles of its products from their inputs to consumption to disposal.[4] Stakeholders expect firms to benchmark their sustainability footprint against such sustainability leaders in their industry.

Several NGOs and organizations rate companies on their environmental and social performance. These include NGOs such as Social Accountability International, financial organizations such as the KLD Social Index, the Jantzi Social Index, and the Dow Jones Sustainability Index, and media outlets such as the Corporate Knights. Consumers and other stakeholders look at these ratings to make decisions about their engagement with the firm. It is better for the firm to proactively provide complete sustainability performance data for these ratings than to be ranked poorly based on incomplete or inaccurate data.

Given evolving societal concerns about a firm's sustainability practices, and the risks and liabilities to shareholders that are inherent in ignoring these concerns, it is important to measure the complete sustainability footprint and then decide which aspects a firm should address via its business model and strategy. The greater the extent to which a firm (and its managers) understand the sustainability performance of its entire value chain, the greater the extent they are prepared to compete for a sustainable future.

Once a firm has a comprehensive picture of its sustainability footprint, it can begin to develop a strategy based on an analysis of:

- The relevance of the various elements of its social and environmental impacts based on the concerns of its salient stakeholders

- The relevance of the various elements of the footprint to the firm's current and future business

- The materiality of various elements of the footprint to its current and future business in terms of inherent risk, license to operate, reputation impacts, cost and revenue implications

- The unique capabilities that can be capitalized to generate future business opportunities and competitive advantage by addressing certain elements of the footprint

While issue-based stakeholder salience and the relevance of elements of the sustainability footprint to the firm's current and future strategy are discussed in this chapter, the link of the sustainability footprint with materiality for the firm is expanded on in Chapter 3. The discussion on unique capabilities is more comprehensively tackled in Chapters 6 and 7.

Relevance of sustainability issues based on stakeholder salience

In order to compete long-term for a sustainable world, a sustainability strategy should never be short term. However, a firm needs to respond immediately to stakeholders that are the most salient to its operations. These stakeholders are salient because they possess one or more of the following three characteristics:[5]

- Power to influence the firm. Power can be coercive, financial or material. That is, a stakeholder may have the ability to affect a firm's sales, and/or its brand image and reputation. Stakeholders such as governments, shareholders, investors, customers, and the media possess this power

- Legitimacy of the relationship of the stakeholder with the firm and the legitimacy of actions of the stakeholder in terms of desirability or appropriateness. For example, shareholders, employees, suppliers, customers, governments, and regulators all have legitimacy in their interactions with the firm. These stakeholders have legal rights attached to their relationship with the firm

- Urgency of the concerns and/or claims of the stakeholders in terms of criticality and time sensitivity. For example, the local community or an NGO may stage a highly visible protest at the firm's facilities, or a customer may file a lawsuit against the firm, or a regulating agency may impose a crippling fine or issue an order for the shutting down of a firm's operations

The salience of a stakeholder group for the firm is determined by the number of attributes—power, legitimacy, and urgency—that the group possesses, and the extent to which it possesses these attributes. A stakeholder group that is legitimate and has the power and urgency of its claim is the highest priority for the firm. Therefore, if a government agency requires the firm to reduce carbon emissions by a certain date, it has the legitimacy, power, and urgency to spur corporate action.

It is important to keep in mind that the three attributes may be gained or lost over time. Moreover, low-priority stakeholders can increase their salience by combining forces with others to boost their power and urgency. For example, an NGO can influence the firm's customers and the media to increase the salience of their claim. Stakeholder salience analysis requires careful planning, guidelines for selection of stakeholders, and background information on the stakeholders and their claims.

Resource dependence. The power of stakeholders to influence the firm's sustainability strategy and practices depends on the resource interdependence between the firm and the specific stakeholders. Stakeholders can influence how a firm uses certain resources. For example, shareholders may demand that their funds be invested only in certain types of projects: whether sustainable or unsustainable. They can withhold further investments or demand repayment or sell the company's shares. Customers can withhold purchasing power and refuse to buy a firm's products or services.[6]

Stakeholders can also use direct or indirect strategies to influence a firm's strategy.[7] In situations of high resource interdependence between the firm and the stakeholder, it is likely that stakeholders will use direct strategies to influence how a firm makes its investments and uses its resources. For example, in the forestry industry, major customers such as construction companies and furniture manufacturers have insisted that the supplier companies obtain certifications based on more sustainable timber harvesting practices[8] such as the Forest Stewardship Council certification.

When stakeholders control critical resources but are not in turn resource dependent on the firm, they would be more likely to use a direct strategy to withhold resources from the firm unless it adopts certain sustainability practices. For example, Canadian regulators have denied licenses to forestry companies to operate on Crown (government) lands unless they adopt sustainable harvesting practices. When the firm and the stakeholders have no resource interdependence on each other, the stakeholders would be likely to exercise indirect strategies via other stakeholders to either influence use of resources that the other stakeholder holds or influence the other stakeholder to withhold the resource from the firm altogether. The type of strategy adopted would depend on whether the stakeholders exercised influence via other stakeholders who, in turn, were resource interdependent with the firm or via those that held stakeholder power. For example, environmental groups have actively participated in environmental assessment hearings in Canada to influence provincial government agencies to deny renewal of Crown leases on forestry lands to firms (an example of an indirect withholding strategy). Environmental groups have also picketed large buyers such as Home Depot and Lowe's in the United States and forced them to change their procurement practices so that they buy wood products only from Canadian companies that adopt sustainable practices (an example of an indirect usage strategy). When the stakeholder group is resource dependent on the firm but the firm has no resource dependence on the stakeholder group (e.g., minor suppliers and easily replaceable employees), the firm's sustainability practices are unlikely to be influenced by stakeholder pressures.

Having identified salient stakeholders based on their power, legitimacy, and urgency, how does the firm decide which elements of its sustainability footprint must be addressed in its immediate strategy and which elements are optional or can be addressed in the future as its long-term strategy? This depends on the sustainability issues that are *important and critical for the salient stakeholders rather than for the firm*. For example, an energy company operating in the Canadian oil sands faces concerns of provincial, national, and international NGOs about its major environmental impacts such as large carbon emissions, massive usage of water, major destruction of habitats, and social issues such as the impacts on traditional livelihoods and quality of life of the Canadian First Nations (aboriginal tribes in the operating area) that constitute the local communities. Even though the operations of the firm are within the provincial and legal regulations in Canada, NGOs and consumers in the US have such major concerns that these issues have been politicized nationally and the US Federal government and several US state governments are opposed to the Keystone XL Pipeline System to transport synthetic crude oil from the oil sands of Alberta, Canada, to refineries in the Gulf Coast of Texas. Even though the pipeline provides a measure of energy independence for the US from tyrannical regimes around that world that it is forced to do business with, the sustainability issues around the pipeline have frozen permissions by the US administration since the first phase from Alberta to Nebraska was built in 2010.[9] Therefore, for a firm operating in the Canadian oil sands, its environmental impacts such as carbon emissions, water usage, water contamination, and habitat destruction are salient issues for NGOs and consumers in the province of Alberta, in Canada, in the US, and internationally, and for the current US federal government and several state governments, in addition to the Canadian national, US, and global media. Obviously, such a firm needs a strategy to address these issues that are important for a large number of salient stakeholders.

A garment manufacturer may have to focus on issues such as a living wage for its workers, their working conditions, and human rights in its supply chain since these are critical issues for international NGOs, its consumers, and the media, especially after the global outrage over the deaths of over a thousand garment workers in a building collapse in Bangladesh.[10] A coffee company may have to develop a strategy to address issues of habitat destruction, fair prices to farmers, and use of chemicals and pesticides, all issues that are important for consumers, NGOs, and media.

Table 2.1 provides a format to analyze the salience of stakeholders concerned about the firm's operations and Table 2.2 provides a format to help the firm assess the relevance of sustainability issues based on the salience of the stakeholders concerned about these issues.

Table 2.1 **Stakeholder salience**

Stakeholders concerned about element of footprint	Stakeholder influence		Salience of stakeholder (high, moderate, low = 15 to 0)			
	Direct	Indirect	Power P	Legitimacy L	Urgency U	Salience S = P + L + U
Shareholders						
Institutional investors						
Regulating agency						
Customers						
Suppliers						
NGOs						
a						
b						
c						
Local community						
Employees						

Table 2.2 **Relevance of issues based on stakeholder salience**

Sustainability footprint of a firm's operations	Stakeholders concerned about footprint element	Salience of stakeholder	Issue relevance to firm's strategy Number of stakeholders (N) × salience (S) R
Environmental footprint			
CO$_2$ emissions			
Other GHG emissions			
Solid waste			
Water quality			
Air quality			
Damage to ecosystem			
Reduced biodiversity of local species			
Social footprint			
Working conditions			
Living wage			
Impact on local employment/traditional livelihoods			
Prices paid to local farmers			
Poverty reduction			
Local entrepreneurship creation			
Displacement of community			

Relevance of sustainability issues to current and future business

Conventional wisdom may suggest to a firm that, for example, carbon emissions, waste water, solid waste, and biodiversity impacts are more relevant for heavy manufacturing and extractive firms; while human rights, fair wages, fair price, and packaging are more relevant for consumer goods and retail firms with supply chains in developing countries; and, energy/material consumption are more relevant for high-tech firms, and so on. While these may be the most relevant impacts for a particular industry or sector, an impact that may seem less relevant could emerge as critical at any stage as *perceived by any of the firm's important stakeholder groups*. For example, Monsanto's genetically modified terminator seed made it impossible for third-world farmers to save seed from their crop for replanting. Monsanto did not consider this a relevant issue for its business and focused on addressing the concerns of regulators and farmers in developed countries. It was only when the global media and NGOs highlighted large-scale demonstrations and protests by farmers in India and other developing countries that Monsanto took notice. At the same time, Monsanto, a US-based company, did not consider the negative attitudes of European consumers toward GMO foods in its strategy.[11] The consequences of ignoring the relevance of these concerns were disastrous for the sales, profitability, and stock price of Monsanto, and thus impacted its business materially.

Similarly, the Wall Street firms were taken by surprise by the "Occupy Wall Street" protests that started in 2011 as disaffected youth connected the 2008 economic downturn and ensuing unemployment to the actions by financial services firms. In fact, the protesters had no demands for the firms and only expressed deep anger against and distrust of the financial sector. The protests generated a great deal of media coverage that led to widespread public reduction in support and trust for the financial services sector across the US and forced politicians to introduce state and federal legislation for stringent regulation of this sector. The protests have not faded away after four years and the movement has become the focal point of anti-corporate and anti-government disaffection in the US.[12] Hence, the Occupy Wall Street movement is a social issue that has relevance for financial firms but the materiality of this issue for firm performance is uncertain at the moment. However, the relevance could translate into materiality if the protests lead to clients withdrawing funds from the firms and regulators enacting new legislation that increases costs for business.

A firm that sells its products exclusively in a small local market will nevertheless have global social and environmental impacts via the inputs and services that it may source from global suppliers, directly or indirectly. Its products may generate greenhouse gases as they are consumed or contribute to landfill waste when they are disposed of. It is possible that its products or the components of its products may be disposed of overseas after use. For example, computers are often shipped at the end of their useful life from richer countries to developing countries. For firms that operate in several countries, and for those that have global supply chains and distribution systems, the sustainability impacts are much more complex due to the number of social and environmental issues that a large number of stakeholders may be concerned about.

During 2009 and 2010, Apple came under fire over working conditions at its major manufacturing contractor Foxconn in China. Allegations were made in several media reports and in an off-Broadway theatrical play purportedly based on factual accounts of working conditions at Foxconn. While some of the reports were exaggerated, a 2012 audit performed by the Fair Labor Association at the behest of Apple found that workers routinely received insufficient overtime pay and workplace accidents were common.[13] There were sixteen suicides at the Foxconn plant during 2009 and 2010, allegedly due to widespread worker abuse and illegal overtime. The TV show, *Nightline,* went inside Foxconn and showed that the company's solution was to install suicide-prevention netting at some facilities rather than address the poor working conditions.[14] Steve Jobs, Apple's CEO at that time, focused on product development, design, and the consumer experience and did not consider working conditions at a contractor's facility to be a relevant issue for Apple's core business. He did not make any public statements to address the public outrage over the issue. In terms of materiality impacts of the social issue, Apple's iPhone began to lose ground to Samsung's Galaxy series in global markets. At this stage, Apple attributed the market share drop purely to product and intellectual property issues. However, after his death, Tim Cook, the new CEO, understood the relevance and materiality of this issue for Apple's stakeholders and consumers and visited a Foxconn plant in central China that employs 120,000 people. At the plant, he declared his intention to eliminate unacceptable labor practices in Apple's supply chain.[15]

It is surprising that Apple took so long to address the issue of working conditions at its contractor's facilities after the many protests by consumers and NGOs about similar issues in corporate supply chains over the last two decades. In the early 1990s Nike came under fire over poor working conditions and exploitation of cheap overseas labor employed in sweatshops manufacturing Nike products. Nike merchandise is manufactured in fifty countries in over 900 factories employing over 660,000 workers. When NGOs and consumers raised the issue of working conditions in the sweatshops, the company did not see the issue as relevant and claimed that the problem lay not with Nike but rather with its contractors. However, this argument did not wash either with NGOs or with consumers. Nike had to assume responsibility. In 1992 it set up a department to monitor human rights and other impacts on social equity in its entire supply chain and established a code of conduct for its suppliers. In 1996 it helped set up the Apparel Industry Partnership to create a code of conduct for contract factories. In 1999, this partnership evolved into an NGO, the Fair Labor Association.[16]

It appears that most companies have yet to internalize the lessons about relevance of social and environmental impacts in their supply chains twenty years after the Nike case and after many other high-profile cases. For example, after over a thousand workers were killed in the Bangladesh garment factory collapse in April 2013, a few manufacturers such as Joe Fresh (a division of Loblaws of Canada), Primark of Britain, and El Corte Ingles of Spain offered compensation for the victims. Others such as Benetton, Mango, Cato, JC Penny, and the Children's Place initially tried to distance themselves from the tragedy. Other companies that rely substantially on third-world contractors, such as Wal-Mart, Gap, H&M, and Carrefour, came together to discuss codes of conduct for outsourcing to Bangladesh.[17] Reflecting the attitudes of their consumers, European retailers were quicker to see the relevance of working conditions in their contractors' factories to their business and to develop strategies to avoid these tragedies in the future, as compared to US companies.[18] However, protests against the non-respondent companies have not died down and continue to affect their sales negatively in some markets.

The examples above refer to instances where direct suppliers are identifiable. Increasingly consumers and other stakeholders are concerned about impacts deeper into the supply chain, that is, the social and environmental impacts of their suppliers' suppliers. It is not always easy to predict which issues stakeholders may choose to express their concerns about in the firm's value chain. As per the example provided above, Apple and Nike had to respond to the concerns of local NGOs focused on human rights and working conditions at its contractors' facilities in China and Indonesia, respectively.

Firms begin by measuring the social and environmental impacts connected to the issues that its primary direct and salient stakeholders are concerned about. This is because a firm perceives that these stakeholders have the power to affect its operational and economic performance. These salient stakeholders usually include customers, regulators, and investors. However, as the examples above show clearly, most firms fail to realize that these primary direct and salient stakeholders are also affected by the concerns of secondary or indirect stakeholders such as the media, local communities, and NGOs.[19]

The material impacts of addressing some aspects of the sustainability footprint are more evident to firms than are others. Many firms have been quick to understand that reducing risk of spills and accidents reduces liability and motivates investors. For example, the *Exxon Valdez* oil spill and BP's *Deepwater Horizon* accident received great publicity and prominence and affected shareholder value of these firms significantly and materially. Most firms have also understood the connection between reducing energy and material use and the cost savings generated and hence higher profitability. Fewer firms understand that fair wages and good working conditions for its employees and its contractors' employees and fair prices paid to suppliers such as commodity farmers in its supply chain all enhance customer preferences and may lead to price premiums and the license to operate in certain jurisdictions. Good relationships with local communities enhance a firm's license to operate and foster favourable assessment of new projects, especially for resource extraction companies. However, it is not always immediately clear to most firms how addressing climate change via reduction in emissions or carbon sequestration affects their economic performance or competitiveness.

Therefore, while regulations, carbon taxes, and societal concerns over climate change due to greenhouse gas accumulation in the Earth's atmosphere have motivated firms in some sectors to assess and reduce their carbon footprint, progress has been slow because managers are uncertain about the materiality of addressing carbon emissions on economic performance. A mining or forestry company may choose to measure impacts on the biodiversity of the habitats it operates in. These impacts are often critical for the major stakeholders of resource extraction firms. Another important area of sustainability impact for mining and forestry companies is the preservation of the traditional livelihood and culture of indigenous populations with historical rights on the land. For example, in Canada most lands on which companies operate are Crown lands that are leased for extraction of natural resources. As a part of the leasing process, firms have to submit detailed plans for addressing social and environmental impacts and have to go through public assessment processes in which any citizen can participate and provide input. Delays in environmental assessment and approval may delay projects for years, leading to escalating costs and lost production and profits.

However, the danger of focusing on sustainability impacts that are perceived to carry high materiality for the business may blindside companies to addressing impacts that may be perceived to be less material but have the potential to generate huge liabilities for business. At the same time, a narrow focus blinds managers to the future business opportunities inherent in areas of impact perceived as less material. While BP focused on investing in its solar panel technology and other forms of renewable energy, it was blindsided by operating flaws in its core oil business that led to massive liabilities as a result of the *Deepwater Horizon* accident in 2010. The estimated total liabilities and payouts for BP as a result of the accident could reach over $90 billion.[20] Issues that have high relevance to a firm's business (such as water and packaging for Coca-Cola) may acquire high materiality if some stakeholders raise the salience of these issues, and sales and profits begin to drop—as happened over the protests over the drop in water tables around a Coca-Cola plant in India and allegations of pesticide contamination in the product.

Nevertheless, many firms begin by measuring one element of their footprint and developing a strategy to reduce the negative impact. Many firms begin by measuring their carbon emissions. This is quite understandable because some European countries and, in 2012, Australia have instituted taxes on carbon emissions or emissions trading schemes, while other jurisdictions are discussing taxes or cap-and-trade schemes. California, often an environmental leader among

US states, introduced a cap-and-trade scheme in 2012.[21] China has begun to tackle its massive pollution levels by initiating discussions about carbon taxes and controls starting in 2013 and has instituted emission reporting by manufacturing operations in 2014.

The focus of this chapter is on helping managers develop an understanding of ways to identify the relevant elements of their sustainability footprint in order to develop an effective sustainability strategy. The chapter does not provide a detailed guide for measuring the sustainability footprint. There are several consulting firms and nonprofit organizations such as the Sustainability Accounting Standards Board[22] and the Global Footprint Network[23] that help nations, regions, cities, and businesses measure their ecological footprint. Larger firms may have in-house resources to measure their social and environmental impacts. While some of these impacts are quite easy to identify, benchmark, and measure, others are much more complex.

A firm's sustainability footprint can be classified very broadly into environmental and social impacts. The section below will outline the relevance of these elements to current and future business and will not elaborate on the various tools used to measure environmental and social footprints of organizations. A description of all the measurement methods and tools would be the subject of another book by itself.

Relevance of the environmental footprint: Impact on ecosystems

The environmental footprint of a firm is a measure of the demands that the activities of the firm, and of its suppliers and consumers, place on the Earth's ecosystems. The Earth's ecosystems have a limited carrying capacity, that is, the size of population of different species, including humans, that the ecosystems can support; the wastes including industrial wastes they can absorb; and the resources (including inputs for industry) they can provide. The environmental footprint represents the burden or strain that the firm imposes on the carrying capacity of the ecosystems. For a manufacturing firm the footprint represents, at the upstream end, the amount of nonrenewable resources and raw materials that it consumes to make its products, and at the downstream end, the quantity of wastes and emissions that are generated in the production, distribution, consumption, and post-use disposal process. As the measurement of the footprint moves beyond the firm's boundaries to its suppliers, its suppliers' suppliers, its distributors, its consumers, and the use and disposal of its product, the footprint gets larger and more difficult to measure. Similarly, for a service company, the footprint considers its inputs (suppliers) and the impacts generated by its consumers. Under the Equator Principles,[24] for example, financial institutions consider the sustainability impacts of the projects that they finance. Generically, the following main categories of environmental impacts need to be considered by companies: impact of wastes on ecosystems; impact of reduced biodiversity on ecosystems; and the impacts of resource extraction on ecosystems.

The impact of wastes on ecosystems

Wastes (often referred to as pollution) are the emissions of gases, solids, and liquid chemicals into air, land, and water, mainly as a result of industrial operations. Many of these chemicals are toxic and hazardous to human health, animal, bird, and fish species, and plant life. These emissions may be the result of normal operations of a firm, or as a result of an industrial accident such as rupture of a pipeline or an oil well (such as the BP *Deepwater Horizon* oil spill in the Gulf of Mexico in 2010), or an accident of a vehicle transporting oil (such as the *Exxon Valdez* oil spill in Prince William Sound, Alaska, in 1989) or accidental discharge of hazardous or toxic chemicals (such as Union Carbide's gas leak at its Bhopal factory in 1984). Environmental regulatory agencies (such as the US Environmental Protection Agency–USEPA) in various countries ban or regulate thousands of chemicals emitted by industrial operations under clean air and water regulations. It is worth noting that many of these chemicals are also emitted as a result of activities of not-for-profit organizations such as government agencies, hospitals, universities, and the armed forces. Wastes from nuclear power plants pose the problems of safe disposal and storage. Some nuclear wastes are radioactive and remain harmful to human health for thousands of years. For example, nuclear fission wastes such as Tc-99 and I-129 have half-lives of 220,000 years and 17 million years, respectively.[25]

Governments usually regulate industrial emissions of wastes and NGOs document pollution levels on public websites to highlight the extent to which different firms or facilities pollute the air and water in their communities. In the US, the EPA requires a disclosure of 682 chemicals and chemical categories under a Toxics Release Inventory (TRI). The TRI lists are publicly available for each manufacturing facility in the US.[26] Similar inventories of wastes are required to be disclosed by several other countries including Canada (the National Pollution Release Inventory[27]) and several European countries. China has introduced reporting requirements for emissions from manufacturing facilities in 2014. Therefore, regulations force firms to measure, report, and track their wastes from year to year. Hence this is usually the first area of measurement focus by firms.

However, consumers and other stakeholders such as environmental NGOs increasingly demand that firms disclose the wastes emitted as a result of the activities of their suppliers and their suppliers' suppliers and so on. Wal-Mart has begun the process of analyzing the sustainability impacts of its 100,000 suppliers and the sustainability impacts along the entire life-cycle of the products it buys and sells.[28] This is an ambitious undertaking that is likely to take several years and significant resource commitments to complete.

In order to be meaningful, measurement of wastes requires not only the creation of an inventory of waste materials but also the inclusion of data on the toxicity of each waste and the negative impacts it has on human health and on air and water purity. Therefore, a smaller quantity of a waste that is ten times as toxic than another waste has a much higher negative environmental impact as compared to another waste that is less than ten times in volume. Many firms also report the *waste intensity* or how much of a specific waste (such as carbon) is generated per unit of production. This enables firms to track improvement over time even if their total production (and hence absolute quantities of wastes) goes up. Critics of measures of waste intensity argue that such a measure allows firms to continue to increase their total absolute negative environmental impact as they increase production, even though they reduce how much waste they generate per unit of production.

An area of waste measurement that has been given a great deal of attention during the last decade is the firm's carbon footprint. This is a complex task. A firm's carbon footprint has two aspects: inputs and outputs. In terms of carbon inputs, a firm's operations may include the direct consumption of fossil fuels (coal, oil, and wood) and the indirect consumption of carbon in its value chain, that is, fossil fuel consumption by its suppliers and transporters; or the deforestation resulting from growing agricultural inputs or for setting up factories that supply inputs to the firm. Deforestation releases carbon dioxide and both agriculture and dairy farming release carbon dioxide and methane. Agriculture is responsible for an estimated 14 percent of the world's greenhouse gases. A significant portion of these emissions come from methane, which, in terms of its contribution to global warming, is 23 times more powerful in trapping heat in the atmosphere as compared to carbon dioxide. A cow emits between 100 to 200 liters per day of methane, almost equal to the pollution produced by a car in a day. In terms of carbon outputs, a firm and/or its distributors, marketers, and consumers (via use of the firm's products) may generate carbon emissions in the form of carbon dioxide and other greenhouse gases in production, transportation, usage, and disposal of its products.

Of course, just as Wal-Mart is attempting to do, developing an effective long-term strategy requires firms to ultimately extend their analysis to the wastes generated by their suppliers and customers along the value chain. At the same time, firms need to benchmark these impacts against sustainability leaders in their industry.

The impact of reduced biodiversity on ecosystems

Biodiversity (biological diversity) is the degree of variation of life forms within a given species, ecosystem, or planet and is a measure of the health of ecosystems. The biodiversity of vegetation, forests, microorganisms, wildlife species, and wetlands in the habitats boosts ecosystem productivity where each species, no matter how small, has an important role to play. A larger number of plant species would result in a greater variety of crops. Greater species diversity ensures natural sustainability for all life forms. Healthy ecosystems can better withstand and recover from a variety of disasters. Mangrove swamps and forests along coastlines absorb a substantial force of hurricanes and protect cities and communities from damage. For example, the intensity of damage caused by Hurricane Katrina would have been substantially reduced if the mangroves on the coastline had not been destroyed. A study showed that areas buffered by coastal mangrove forests were less damaged by the massive 2004 tsunami in the Pacific Ocean than areas without tree vegetation.[29]

While the reduction or elimination of wastes helps reduce negative impacts on habitats within which firms operate, biodiversity within the habitats can continue to be affected negatively. Regulators and stakeholders such as local communities, indigenous people, environmental NGOs, and consumers may be concerned about the impacts of the firm's operations on the biodiversity of habitats. They may demand that a firm restore damage to the habitats and their biodiversity as a consequence of the firm's activities.

Mining and resource extraction companies have a significantly neg-ative impact on habitat biodiversity. For example, firms in Alberta, Canada, engaged in the mining of tar sands and the production of oil from these sands cause significant damage to the biological and recreational value of land and the ecosystems in the mining area. In addition, combustion and thermal processing using large quantities of natural gas generate massive wastes. These firms use millions of gallons of water and create vast lakes of toxic tailings that destroy wildlife and damage the ecosystem. Recent expansion of shale oil pro-duction using the hydraulic fracturing of sub-strata rock formation (or "fracking") has generated a great deal of debate about dangers to ecosystems. Fracking is a water-intensive process where millions of gallons of fluid—typically a mix of water, sand, and chemicals—are injected underground at high pressure to fracture the rock surround-ing an oil or gas well. This releases extra oil and gas from the rock, so it can flow into the well. But the process of fracking damages habitats due to clearing of land to build new access roads and new well sites, drilling and encasing the well, fracking the well and generating the waste, trucking in heavy equipment and materials, and trucking out the large quantities of toxic waste. These contribute to air and water pollution risks and devaluation of land values. Several communities and states such as Vermont in the US and Quebec in Canada and several countries (such as France) have banned fracking. In others countries such as the UK, opposition to fracking is widespread, in the face of which several firms have shut down drilling operations.[30]

Biodiversity is not easy to measure, based on the expertise available in-house in businesses. Large resource extraction firms employ biolo-gists and zoologists who help measure and track the diversity of ani-mal and plant life and the health of water bodies and soil over time. Smaller firms have to rely on consultants with expertise in measuring ecosystem biodiversity. Such experts can also help the firm measure impacts on biodiversity along its value chain. Ultimately, firms need a good understanding of their impacts on biodiversity if they have to develop an effective competitive strategy for a sustainable future.

The impact of resource extraction on ecosystems

The Earth's resources are finite. Several stakeholders are concerned about the sustained availability of these resources for future generations. The Earth's forests, fisheries, water bodies, groundwater, soil, and minerals are being depleted at a rapid pace and numbers of plant and animal species are fast approaching extinction. As the world's human population grows, there is concern about how these larger populations with increasing nutrition demands will be fed and whether we will have enough clean water and enough raw materials to produce the products and services in order to maintain increasingly affluent lifestyles. The problem of material, energy, and resource scarcity is exacerbated as large emerging middle-class populations in developing economies aspire to consume like affluent Western consumers.

The beneficial effect of reduced and/or more efficient use of materials is lower pressure on escalating world prices for commodities, lower input costs for businesses, and lower wastes. Reduction of wastes represents an immediate financial benefit because waste is *the proportion of input resources that is not transformed into finished products*. This is clearly an opportunity for business both in terms of a short-term and long-term strategy rather than a threat to its operations.

Firms measure material and energy intensity to track how material and energy input per unit of production is being reduced over time. Firms can also track the proportion of renewable materials (for example, use of biomass instead of virgin old-growth forests) and renewable energy sources (for example, solar and wind instead of oil and coal) that they substitute for nonrenewable materials and energy sources.

Relevance of the social footprint: Impact on society

The social footprint of a firm is a measure of the impacts its operations and the operations of its suppliers and customers (and its entire value chain) have on society. For example, a business's operations may impact positively or negatively on:

- Employee welfare, safety and health

- Culture, heritage, lifestyle, and economic welfare of local communities

- Living wage, working conditions, and human rights, such as the rights of women and minorities to work and earn a fair wage and the right of children to an education. These impacts ripple through the firm's value chain including impacts on the employees of the firm's contractors and of its suppliers and retailers

- Income and/or quality of life of marginalized societies including those eking out a living at less than a dollar a day, specifically as they may relate to inputs grown, harvested, and manufactured by the very poor. The fair trade movement emphasizes that fair prices should be paid to suppliers, especially low income and marginal farmers

The social footprint may be visualized as social impacts radiating outward from the core of the firm: from employees to local communities within which the firm operates, to growers of basic materials that go into inputs to communities affected by the disposal of products after use.

The impact on employee welfare and quality of life

The firm needs to start by measuring its social impacts at the core of its operations: on its employees' welfare, health, safety, working conditions, and quality of life (including the right to a living wage). Firms promote wellness programs and disease prevention, such as AIDS prevention programs, in some jurisdictions. They measure the decline in workplace accidents year on year and aspire to a zero accident rate. They implement diversity programs to provide equal opportunities to all segments of society and offer benefits such as parental leave, healthcare, same sex benefits, and childcare facilities. This is an area in which many firms have developed leading practices. Social impacts are measured via safety records and employee benefits as compared to industry standards, employee turnover and loyalty, absenteeism, and wellness. This is a critical area for a firm to tackle immediately. Any long-term sustainability strategy will not be seen as credible if the employees are not provided good working conditions and a living wage.

The impact on local communities

The next layer the firm needs to look at is the local communities that it operates in. Involvement with local communities is sometimes referred to as corporate citizenship or corporate community relations. A major contribution that the firm makes to the community is to generate employment and taxes that help fund social welfare and quality of life within the communities. Often, communities and entire towns grow around manufacturing facilities. For example, firms that are a part of the Tata Group of Companies of India have developed entire towns around major manufacturing facilities. The city of Jamshedpur (current population 1.3 million) was established as a planned industrial city around the Tata Steel Company in 1908. Firms also contribute philanthropically to local schools, hospitals, sports teams or little leagues, shelters for the homeless and for abused women, and other social projects. Firms that operate on lands where indigenous communities have rights to live and earn livelihood often develop strategies to engage these communities for economic benefit. For example, mining and forestry firms sometimes help members of indigenous communities become entrepreneurs and integrate them into their supply chains.

Firms may measure community complaints and disputes on the one hand, and community engagement and support on the other.

Generally, it can be assumed that the higher the gap between positive actions for community engagement and negative disputes and
complaints, the higher the firm's *license to operate*. Firms may also
measure social welfare indicators in communities such as changes in
per capita income and comparative indicators of health, education,
and communication access versus averages for the country they operate in or for similar sets of countries.

Addressing the concerns of civil society

Nongovernmental organizations are representations of civil society
that emerge to address social issues not addressed by government or
business. While many NGOs are local or are easy to identify, it is
possible that environmental and social NGOs operating in distant
locations may be concerned about the firm's operations or those of
its suppliers. For example, NGOs in China raised concerns about
working conditions in Apple's contractor Foxconn and Indonesian
NGOs began a campaign against working conditions in the factories of Nike's contractors; this latter campaign spread to NGOs in
the developed world and to Nike's consumers.[31] In another instance,
in 1995, German Greenpeace started a campaign against Shell UK's
plans to dispose its offshore oil platform, the *Brent Spar*, in the North
Atlantic, even though Germany does not have offshore oil rigs and
this was initially an issue far from the consciousness of the German
people.[32]

Firms need to develop systems for identifying not only the visible or
core stakeholders but also the distant stakeholders or those connected
to the distant stakeholders at the fringe of stakeholder networks.[33]
Firms can measure the opposition from, and conflict with, NGOs versus their support and engagement to get a net measure of *stakeholder
legitimacy*.

Raising the base of the pyramid

The concept of sustainable development as stated by the Brundtland Commission Report urged equity across social groups and across generations. Such equity requires the reduction in the immense disparities that exist between rich and poor. Firms face the challenge of developing sustainable business models that alleviate poverty and create economic opportunities when they operate at the base of the pyramid, that is, in contexts where people earn less than one or two dollars a day. Such contexts are often referred to as the bottom of the pyramid[34] or the base of the pyramid (BOP), to reflect the potential of these contexts as the foundation (base) for reverse innovation and sustainable business models, rather than as the bottom of the economic heap as implied in World Bank economic reports. BOP contexts need to be considered separately from developed or middle-income markets that firms normally operate in, because they are very different in terms of income levels, consumption levels, culture, and infrastructure. Usually these contexts are located in emerging and poor markets with extreme poverty levels. Generating a positive social impact in such contexts requires business models that are significantly different from those in developed countries. Such business models often require co-creation of products and business models with communities in these countries to generate a deep understanding of their fundamental needs.[35]

Impacts in BOP contexts are measured via community welfare in terms of raising income levels, distribution of income, health and hygiene, education, availability of clean water, access to markets, and communication. Corporate engagement in a radically different business context such as the base of the pyramid also has the potential to lead to innovative new technologies, processes, products, services, and business models. For example, the Grameen Bank business model of micro-lending to the poor has been adopted in the US initially via Shore Bank and subsequently via Grameen America. Similarly, in response to the dispersed rural population needs and the lack of a healthcare infrastructure, GE Healthcare developed a portable, battery-run scanning and imaging machine called the Vscan in India. The Vscan is transported by medical technicians on motorcycles to the smallest of villages for health checks and diagnosis. This technology is now being transferred to developed markets as a low-cost alternative for dispersed and rural populations.[36] Developing sustainable business models at the base of the pyramid will be discussed in more depth in Chapter 7.

The above discussion explains how, based on the salience of the stakeholders concerned about a firm's environmental and social impact, it is possible to identify relevant issues that should be at the core of a firm's sustainability strategy. Based on the salience of these stakeholders and the degree of resource dependence of the firm on the stakeholders, the firm can identify the relevance and impact of these sustainability issues to its current and future business. That is, if customers are concerned about a firm's carbon dioxide emissions, it is not enough to simply reduce emissions in line with regulations and clean air standards; it is also necessary to evolve a long-term strategy to develop products and services based on a low carbon footprint to take advantage of these consumers and markets. Table 2.3 provides a format that firms can use to analyze the impact of an issue to its current and future business. This is only a preliminary step. Developing a long-term competitive sustainable strategy for the future requires building logic, motivations, and capabilities. These are elaborated in the following chapters.

Table 2.3 **Impact of issue on current and future business (high, moderate, low = 5 to 0)**

	Issue relevance based on total stakeholder salience R	Issue relevance to existing business (Table 2.2) E	Potential impact on current sales and profits IE	Short-term relevance STR (E+IE)	Relevance to future business F	Potential impact on future sales and profits IF	Long-term relevance LTR (F+IF)
Environmental footprint							
CO_2 emissions							
Other GHG emissions							
Solid waste							
Water quality							
Air quality							
Damage to ecosystem							
Biodiversity of local species							
Social footprint							
Working conditions							
Living wage							
Impact on local employment/							
Traditional livelihoods							
Prices paid to local farmers							
Poverty reduction							
Local entrepreneurship creation							
Displacement of community							

Summary

Firms often focus on measuring one element or a few elements of their sustainability footprint, such as carbon emissions. However, it is important to obtain a comprehensive picture of a firm's footprint before developing a strategy to compete in a sustainable world. This is because some impacts considered less relevant and material may emerge as critical at some stage and significantly affect the firm's economic performance or survival. At the same time, an incomplete picture makes it more difficult for managers to identify potential business opportunities that may lie at the intersections of various environmental and social impacts.

A firm's environmental footprint measures the stress it places on the Earth's ecosystems by generating wastes and emissions (including carbon), affecting biodiversity of life, and drawing on nonrenewable resources for its inputs and energy consumption. Its social footprint radiates outward from the core of the organization in terms of employee safety and welfare, local community economic health and social welfare, responsiveness to the concerns of core and fringe stakeholders, and generating positive social impacts at the base of the pyramid. Before developing a strategy, a firm needs to assess the salience of stakeholders concerned about the various elements, the relevance of the various elements to its business, and the impact of the element for its current and future business. It is important for firms to understand that an issue that has low relevance may become more relevant over time, an issue with high relevance may acquire high materiality over time, and therefore this assessment needs to be a dynamic process.

Most firms begin by engaging external consultants to set up systems for measuring, monitoring, and benchmarking their environmental and social footprints. They also get these measures audited regularly by a third-party firm to establish the credibility of the data. They benchmark themselves against firms considered sustainability leaders and establish goals for reducing their negative footprint and building an increasingly positive footprint year on year. Leading firms also report on their progress via sustainability reports to their stakeholders in order to demonstrate their seriousness and commitment by allocating resources for sustainability practices and making positive progress on the measured indicators.

In order to identify innovative sustainability practices and strategies, employees need to be involved at all levels. They need to be provided with regular information about the firm's progress along these goals. Once employees monitor their firm's progress over time, and understand the risks of not adopting sustainability practices, it is easier to enable them to build a business case for sustainability.

Three
Sustainable strategy and competitive advantage

Properly focused, the profit motive can accelerate (not inhibit) the transformation toward global sustainability.

Stuart L. Hart, *Capitalism at the Crossroads*, Pearson Education, Inc., Upper Saddle River, New Jersey

Firms attain competitive advantage by consistently achieving higher than average profits or returns on investment as compared to other firms in their industry. Firms can attain competitive advantage either by consistently delivering value to consumers at costs lower than their competitors can, or by differentiating their product and service offerings from their competitors, enabling them to sell more and command premium prices, or via a combination of the two strategies.[37] Differentiation refers to the distinctiveness of a firm's products and services that translates into customer preference to buy from that firm or to pay a premium price for its products and services over those of its competitors. As increasing numbers of customers become concerned about the social and environmental footprint of a firm, its sustainability practices and impacts become important differentiating attributes that influence the consumer decision.

Consistently maintaining low costs or differentiation against the onslaught of competition requires continuous innovation in cost effectiveness, improved processes and products, and new products, services and business models that displace those of competitors or create brand-new markets. As radical innovations emerge and industries are disrupted, the competitive boundaries in the industry may change. For example, the iPad created an entirely new industry but also competed against conventional laptop computers and PDA devices. A sustainable strategy has the potential to reorient organizational processes to generate such innovations and generate competitive advantage in a variety of ways that are discussed in this chapter.

Societal demands that corporations respond to global sustainability challenges comprise a major change in the operating environment of business over the past couple of decades. Such demands present risks as well as opportunities for business. Firms need to develop strategies to compete and succeed in this changed environment. A survey by Accenture in 2010 revealed that CEOs of leading global corporations recognize that societal concern for business sustainability is not a fad but an accelerating trend. The CEOs also recognize that a sustainable strategy is the basis of future corporate value and competitive advantage. The CEOs in the Accenture study understand well that there is increasing societal concern over issues such as climate change, extinction of species, degradation of habitats, escalating prices of food and commodities, chronic poverty, and greater inequality in distribution of income, all trends that are accelerating and will continue to do so in the near future.[38] The intensity of societal concern on a specific issue may wax or wane but overall generally exhibits an upward trend. For example, societal concern about greenhouse gas emissions (specifically, carbon dioxide) has consistently increased over the past two decades in spite of continuing media debate (and a skeptical political lobby, notably in the US) over the role of fossil fuels in impacting climate change.

Civil society in the form of NGOs has grown at a rapid rate during the past three decades to address the sustainability challenges and social injustices not addressed by business and governments. According to some estimates, there are several million NGOs around the world, many of them focused on social and environmental issues. According to Wikipedia, there are an estimated 1.5 million NGOs operating in the US, 277,000 in Russia, and around 3.3 million in India.[39] Even in rich developed countries there are increasing concerns about social inequalities and calls for more stringent regulation of the financial services industry. This reached a climax during the financial crisis of 2008 with increasing concern about the increasing gap between rich and poor and eroding social equity in the world's richest country, the United States, and widespread irresponsible and unethical practices by individuals in several financial institutions. These societal concerns spawned movements such as Occupy Wall Street in the US in 2011 and similar protest movements in other countries.

Such societal concerns present business risks and could create conditions that may threaten the economic viability of certain industries. At the same time, by addressing these concerns effectively via innovative business models, products, and services, firms could potentially find ways to reduce costs, differentiate their offerings, and find new business opportunities that can generate competitive advantage in the short and long term. Each opportunity for action on an element of a firm's social and/or environmental footprint discussed in Chapter 2 also presents a threat in the form of the business risks of ignoring that impact. Managers can make more informed decisions to develop effective strategies if they have a good understanding of both: the business risks of ignoring stakeholder concerns about social and environmental impacts; and the competitive benefits of developing a proactive sustainability strategy to identify and capitalize on opportunities. These are two sides of the same coin: by reducing the risks of not addressing their negative social and environmental impacts, firms also have the potential to find opportunities for cost reduction, differentiation, and imagination for future products, services, and business models. This chapter describes how addressing each of these risks leads to benefits for business and potential sources of short-term and long-term competitive advantage.

Cost advantages of pollution prevention

In terms of managing the air (gases), land (solid), and water (emissions) pollution and wastes generated, firms have responded in the following ways with consequences for risk reduction and cost advantage.

The risks and costs of noncompliance

In some jurisdictions where the fines are not punitive and directors are not subject to criminal liability, a firm may be noncompliant and continue to emit wastes disallowed by regulations. This is a breach of regulations and therefore certainly not endorsed or suggested in this book. However, it is a fact that in some jurisdictions, in the absence of stringent penalties, some firms prefer to pay the fines rather than invest in expensive pollution control. In many other jurisdictions, environmental regulations mandate civil (and sometimes criminal) penalties for the board of directors and senior executives for noncompliance. Wherever financial penalties are accompanied by imprisonment of directors, firms are not tempted to adopt a noncompliance approach.

Cost disadvantages of pollution control

Many firms clean up pollution to the minimum extent required by law. Firms are required to comply with regulations that apply to the manufacture, use, disposal, and release of chemical substances and to other activities that adversely affect the environment. They may be required to remedy sites or habitats damaged by their operations. This applies significantly to natural resource extraction businesses. They may be required to compensate individuals for personal injury, property damage, and economic loss. For example, firms usually install pollution control equipment such as electrostatic precipitators (also known as scrubbers) in smokestacks to reduce air emissions such as sulfur dioxide to within regulatory limits and effluent treatment plants to remove

toxic contaminants from discharged water. Compliance with regulations by adopting technologies prescribed by regulators to control
and clean up pollution requires substantial investments. Other than in
avoiding the fines and penalties of noncompliance, these investments
do not pay back.

Installing pollution control equipment may reduce the risks associated with noncompliance with federal, state and local regulations.
However, it does not shield a firm from emergent environmental liabilities due to accidents, changing regulations, or actions by private
citizens and communities. These liabilities oblige the firm to allocate
resources to remedy its environmental impacts or incur substantial
legal costs to defend its operations against penalties and fines. In some
jurisdictions, such as Alberta, firms in the oil industry have been sued
for damage to health of humans and cattle and other animals as a
result of lawful discharge of sour gas as a by-product of oil drilling. A
firm's directors and senior managers may be held criminally liable for
deaths of humans and animal species caused by toxic emissions. For
example, Warren Anderson, the former CEO of Union Carbide, and
his company faced criminal charges of multiple culpable homicides
in India after the gas leak at the company plant in Bhopal in 1984.[40]
Similarly, Captain Hazelwood of Exxon faced criminal charges for
the *Exxon Valdez* oil spill in 1989.[41] Firms may be required to pay
punitive damages as a result of grossly negligent conduct or pay for
damage to common natural resources such as the estimated $90 bil-
lion total liability associated with BP's *Deepwater Horizon* oil rig
blowout in 2010.[42]

Not only are environmental liabilities generated as a result of existing laws, they also often emerge as a result of new regulations that are
constantly being enacted or existing regulations that are being made
more stringent. The costs of compliance may range from administrative requirements (e.g., recordkeeping, reporting, labeling, and
employee training) to more substantial capital costs for pre-treating
wastes prior to disposal or to scrub air emissions. Costs may also
relate to exiting a site or business, such as proper closure of waste

disposal sites and post-closure monitoring. For example, the cost of safely decommissioning a nuclear power reactor at the end of its useful life may range from 400 million dollars to well over a billion dollars.

Similarly, remediation liabilities may include excavation, drilling, construction, pumping, soil and water treatment, and monitoring of closed-down sites. The remediation and reclamation costs of closed-down mines and production facilities can significantly affect a firm's bottom line. Remediation costs may also require that the firm provide safe drinking water supplies for communities whose water supplies are affected by its operations. Large-scale projects may require a firm to relocate entire communities and develop an infrastructure for such communities. Remediation also requires the hiring of experts to conduct technical studies, and the costs of management, professional, and legal resources. The company may face remediation obligations long after it has abandoned a site. In fact, under the US Comprehensive Environmental Response, Compensation and Liability Act (CERCLA or the "Superfund" Act), a firm is liable for contamination in an inactive site that it may have owned formerly but does not own now, at a property it never owned or used but to which its wastes were sent, and even at a contaminated property it acquired but did not contaminate.[43]

In addition to punitive and deterrent fines and penalties, firms may have a liability to pay for compensation of damages suffered by individuals, their property, and businesses due to use or release of toxic substances or other pollutants. These liabilities may occur even if a company is in compliance with all applicable environmental standards. Thus, the discharge of sour gas from oil wells in Alberta is within the limits regulated but nevertheless the damage to health is subject to civil litigation. Thus firms could be liable for personal injury (e.g., wrongful death, bodily injury, medical monitoring, pain and suffering), property damage (e.g., diminished value of real estate, buildings, or automobiles; loss of crops), and economic loss (e.g., lost profits, cost of renting substitute premises or equipment). In addition, liabilities incur legal defense costs (potentially including technical, scientific, economic, and medical studies) even when the claims are ultimately determined to be without merit. Moreover, responding to compensation claims can consume management time and require expenditures in order to control damage to corporate image. The compensation liabilities may be supplemented by punitive damages awarded by the court to punish and deter conduct viewed as callous disregard for others. These may be many times larger than the costs of compensation. As described above, these damages are common in instances such as the *Exxon Valdez* oil spill, the Bhopal tragedy, and BP's *Deepwater Horizon* oil spill.

US regulations such as the Clean Water Act, the CERCLA or "Superfund" Act, and the Oil Pollution Act (OPA) hold firms liable for injury, destruction, loss, or loss of use of natural resources that do not constitute private property but rather those controlled by federal, state, local, foreign, or tribal governments. Such resources include flora, fauna, land, air, and water resources. The liability can arise from accidental releases (e.g., during transport) as well as lawful releases to air, water, and soil.

Compliance with regulations via pollution control is no guarantee that environmental accidents will not occur. Such accidents can still lead to huge liabilities, civil suits by citizens and communities, and also potentially fines or prison terms for members of the board and senior managers of the firm. For example, compliance with regulations did not prevent accidents such as BP's *Deepwater Horizon* oil spill and the ensuing liability and civil and criminal lawsuits. The BP accident has resulted in a criminal settlement with the US government of $5.4 billion but the estimates for civil claims could be in the range of $90 billion. BP has also been barred from bidding on US government contracts. This does not consider the substantial loss of sales and damage to BP's corporate reputation.[44] Investors saw the value of their stock holdings in BP shrink by 54 percent in 2010.[45] Moreover, environmental accidents such as spills of chemicals or rupture of pipelines or oil wells or gas/chemical blowouts at manufacturing facilities can no longer be insured. Such accidents could lead to massive financial liabilities that could potentially end in bankruptcy for a firm. The gas leak and explosion at the Union Carbide chemical factory in Bhopal in 1984 led to the bankruptcy and break-up of the company. The *Exxon Valdez* oil spill in Prince William Sound in Alaska in 1989 led to large liabilities and a significant drop in Exxon's sales and shareholder value for a period of time.

Organizations have to be wary that civil and criminal law is constantly evolving to include environmental and social impacts of companies. Prior to the grounding of the *Exxon Valdez,* there was no precedent of criminal penalties for maritime accidents caused through errors of navigation or management of a vessel. Similarly, the international maritime law was changed after Greenpeace protests over the plans for the first-ever disposal of an offshore oil rig, the *Brent Spar*, in the North Atlantic by Shell UK.[46] Currently, even though hydraulic fracturing ("fracking") to extract shale gas is legal in most US states, there is a fast-growing multi-stakeholder movement to ban fracking. Several US states such as Vermont, the province of Quebec in Canada, and most European countries have banned it. Even though fracking is not banned in the UK, there is strong and widespread opposition in the country.[47]

Therefore, it is clear that compliance as a strategy leads to a cost *disadvantage* and will not enable the firm to cope with changing regulations, changing societal and consumer concerns, and human error.

The cost advantages of pollution prevention

Proactive practices to prevent pollution at source substantially can reduce the requirement to invest in compliance and hence can save substantial costs[48] for a firm. A firm can prevent pollution at source by rethinking and altering processes to eliminate or substantially reduce the generation of solid, liquid, and/or gaseous waste emissions. This approach, often referred to as P2 (Pollution Prevention), requires investments that pay back via two types of cost savings. It reduces or eliminates the capital costs of pollution control equipment that are unlikely to yield any return on the investment other than reducing legal penalties for noncompliance. It also enables the transformation of a higher percentage of raw inputs into finished product. Waste is a representation of inputs that do not realize value in the market but are discarded and may actually cost the firm significantly for safe disposal as per regulations. Reduced waste means greater production and higher sales and profits.

Firms have collectively saved billions of dollars by preventing pollution at source during the last four decades, starting in the 1970s. For firms that still need to make a business case for such investments, it is relevant to highlight the potential costs savings by pointing to some well-known examples of corporate programs that have generated substantial savings via pollution prevention at source. As far back as 1975, 3M initiated its 3P program (Pollution Prevention Pays). In its first year, the program undertook nineteen projects that prevented 73,000 tons of air emissions and 2,800 tons of chemical sludge. During the thirty-five years since the inception of the program, 3P has resulted in the elimination of more than 3.5 billion pounds of pollution and saved nearly $1.5 billion in costs.[49] Similarly, Dow Chemical Company's WRAP (Waste Reduction Always Pays) program has reduced 230,000 tons of raw material, 13 million tons of water, 8 trillion BTU' of energy, 1.6 billion pounds of solid waste, 25 percent of greenhouse gas emissions, and over $9.2 billion in energy costs since 1994.[50] DuPont has reduced wastes and energy usage by 80 percent since 1990 and this has resulted in savings of $3 billion for the firm.[51]

The examples provided above are for chemical companies. However, similar principles apply to most other industries as well—reducing wastes reduces costs. For example, between 1985 and 1995, Intel increased revenues from $1.8 billion to $12 billion and reduced its wastes from 5,000 tons to 1,500 tons, a 70 percent reduction in overall waste generation for an almost sevenfold increase in sales.[52] Since then, Intel has made continuous progress on reduction of emissions, wastes, and energy use, and conservation of water. IBM's semiconductor fabrication plant in Essex, Vermont, has generated substantial savings by reducing its energy use by over 30 percent between 2007 and 2012 while increasing its production during the same period.[53] In October 2013, the Essex facility of IBM received the IBM's Most Valuable Pollution Prevention (MVP2) award from the US National Pollution Prevention Roundtable for the development of a manufacturing process that reduces IBM's greenhouse gas use by nearly 12,000 metric tons annually.[54] However, the primary motivation of energy reduction has been not so much pollution reduction but rather cost reduction and competitiveness of the facility.

An interesting example of solid waste reduction is the diversion of filters from landfills by the petroleum industry. The petroleum industry uses vast quantities of filters to clean oil at the wellhead, during transportation in pipelines, and during refining. These filters were originally disposed of in landfills. However, during the late 1980s and early 1990s, several communities in Alberta, Canada and some US states complained about the trace oil in these filters leaching from landfills into the groundwater. The trace oil contaminated the water bodies that were sources of drinking water for cattle (Alberta's second largest industry is cattle ranching and beef) and from which the farms tapped their drinking water. The protests resulted in provincial regulations to ban the disposal of used oil filters and oil-absorbent materials in landfills since trace oil from filters could leak and contaminate water bodies. Several US states also began to ban the landfill disposal of used oil filters. The various state and provincial environmental regulatory agencies prescribed several costly methods for disposal ranging from draining the oil from filters before they were recycled or disposed of—a costly, laborious, and time-consuming process, lining the trucks in which the filters were transported with thick plastic sheets, lining the landfills where they were disposed of with plastic sheets to prevent leakage, and building concrete catchment pits to collect any oil that leaked. Facing significant costs of meeting these regulations, one firm hit upon a simple solution to prevent this pollution. It began crushing these filters in one location and sending the separated metal and trace oil for recycling, thereby eliminating the costs of transportation and disposal. The filters also became revenue generators from the metal scrap and oil recycling industries. This investment quickly paid back in saved costs and revenues and soon became standard industry practice. Therefore, pollution prevention often requires some innovative thinking to come up with simple low-cost solutions that generate substantial cost savings.

An interesting example of solid waste prevention was presented at a conference by Dr. Paul Tebo, former Senior Vice President for Environment, Health and Safety at DuPont.[55] Chad Holliday, DuPont's CEO, established a goal of zero solid waste for DuPont's manufacturing facilities. The objective was to harness the ingenuity of employees to generate zero waste solutions. Given the goal of zero solid waste at its Corian division that produced laminate sheets for counter tops, the plant's managers were able to make significant reductions in waste through greater efficiency and process and quality control. After reaching a certain level of efficiency they hit a wall. Further investments led to very minor or incremental reduction in waste. A percentage of the waste was due to tiny impurities that appeared as specks in solid single-color sheets of plastic. These sheets could not be sold and were sent to the landfill because the customers demanded blemish-free sheets for counter tops. Moreover, this was standard industry practice. Pressed for zero waste solutions, the plant's managers hit upon an idea to add different colors to create patterns and swirls that accentuated the specks that were previously considered impurities. They were thus able to reduce most of the solid waste. Pushed further to reduce solid waste absolutely to zero, they began to sell the waste trimmings from the sheets to manufacturers of pens and key chains and other plastic-covered accessories that could wrap these trimmings around their products. Hence, the goal of zero solid waste was achieved as a result of setting an ambitious stretch goal and relying on employee ingenuity.

Pollution prevention also reduces insurance costs. As a result of climate change, weather patterns are less predictable and insurance companies are increasingly reluctant to underwrite weather-related risks. Even when these risks are undertaken, the premiums come at a prohibitive cost. Insurance companies rarely, if ever, insure environmental accidents such as oil spills and toxic chemical accidents. Firms have to self-insure such risks. For example, accidents such as the *Deepwater Horizon* oil spill in 2010, that has been estimated to cost BP around 90 billion dollars in liabilities, will have to be generated internally. Similarly, the Bhopal toxic chemical spill that killed and injured thousands led to lawsuits and legal liabilities that eventually resulted in the bankruptcy of Union Carbide. A proactive sustainability strategy avoids such crippling liabilities and insurance costs.

Cost savings from pollution prevention are easy wins and low-hanging fruit that firms can reap, often with insubstantial investments, creativity and ingenuity. However, such costs savings suffer from diminishing returns. As the wastes are eliminated, potential cost savings are eliminated as well. At the same time, competing firms can easily catch up by adopting similar pollution prevention practices and strategies. Therefore, pollution prevention is a cost advantage strategy in an early stage of a firm's sustainability strategy.

Cost advantage and differentiation via eco-efficiency and product or process redesign

Natural resources are major inputs for manufacturing and service industries. While manufacturing industries transform these resources into finished products, service industries such as skiing and tourism rely on these resources for their business. Extraction of natural resources by mining, forestry, and fishing firms, for example, and exploitation of the environment leads to the degradation of physical resources, threatening the viability and existence of several industries. As the organic value of soil degrades due to the intensified use of chemicals and fertilizers, yields are threatened. As groundwater aquifers decline due to intensive irrigation (for example, in the US midWest, known as the wheat bowl), world food supplies are threatened.

As fisheries and forests disappear, entire industries become extinct and several indigenous communities lose their livelihood. As non-renewable materials are intensively extracted, commodities become scarce and prices move upward, threatening the viability of several industries dependent on these inputs. As global warming reduces the extent and period of snow cover, the skiing industry is threatened and agricultural industries dependent on snow melt for water flow could become extinct. Various other industries such as tourism and real estate are affected by environmental degradation.

A reduction in the use of natural resources (material and energy) as inputs is achieved not only via pollution prevention but also via eco-efficiency and the redesign of processes and products. This not only enhances the long-term survival of business, but also generates significant costs savings and could lead to differentiated products, services, and business models.

Dematerialization

While reduction in process waste reduces the quantity of material required to produce the same quantity of a product, process and product design innovations can lead to reduced use of materials as well. This translates into improvement in productivity and process efficiency since a higher percentage of input is converted into finished product. The early applications of dematerialization were via the use of reduced or recycled packaging and reducing multiple layers of packaging that was redundant for product protection. The German packaging laws, implemented in three phases between 1991 and 1993, were pioneering legislations in this regard. The laws forced businesses to redesign their products for complete recycling or disassembly and take-back. Some firms were surprised to find that the process generated cost savings and quick returns on investment. As a consequence of the redesign German auto firms such as BMW and Volkswagen developed unique capabilities of 100 percent disassembly of their vehicles at the end of use.

Since then, many firms have achieved dematerialization through a variety of ways, including recycling and re-use, product and process redesign, miniaturization, product/service substitution, and integration of environmental considerations into total quality control processes. These are briefly touched upon below.

Recycling and re-use

Recycling can take the form of use of the waste of one firm by another firm. For example, IBM recycles its discarded and defective wafers; 250,000 silicon wafers are started each day in the world, and IBM estimates that about 3.3 percent of the wafers are scrapped. At its Essex, Vermont, fabrication facility, by recycling its scrapped wafers as monitor wafers, IBM saves over $1.5 million a year. IBM also sells its defective wafers to solar cell manufacturers. By using recycled silicon, solar cell manufacturers can save between 30 percent and 90 percent of the energy they normally use in creating solar cells, thus lowering the carbon footprint of their products.[56] Firms have also generated substantial cost savings by re-using the wastes that they generate. For example, the construction industry increasingly re-uses larger quantities of its waste, such as brick, wood, steel, and asphalt, resulting in substantial cost savings.

It is important to recognize that recycling does not always lead to cost savings for the firm, and sometimes it does not lead to a net reduction in the environmental footprint. A cost-benefit analysis may be necessary before a firm develops a strategy to use recycled material. For example, in the manufacture of newspapers different jurisdictions and certifications mandate a certain recycled content. In order to satisfy these regulations or certifications, firms may spend more energy in collection of waste paper than they may save in the manufacturing process by using the recycled material. In some US states, post-consumer recycled newsprint has to be brought in from Canada and Mexico because several US states do not have recycling laws or practices. In its 1988 Comprehensive Purchasing Guidelines for federal agency purchasing, EPA required a minimum of 40 percent post-consumer fiber in newsprint, consistent with the requirements of several of the states pushing recycled newsprint laws or agreements at the time. But in its 1995 revisions to the paper purchasing requirements, EPA dropped its minimum for newsprint from 40 percent to 20 percent. The reason for the change was that surveys of paper manufacturers indicated that the actual amount of post-consumer waste they were using averaged only 20 percent, with the rest of the recycled content made up of pre-consumer printing and the conversion of scraps.

Product redesign

A product can be redesigned to make it lighter and smaller, thus using less material. Procter & Gamble is well-known for reformulating its washing detergents and cleaning products into higher concentrations, significantly reducing the packaging and increasing value for the customer. Other examples of product redesign include the reformulation of lighter and stronger materials such as carbon composite steels, plastics, and fiberglass for cars, boats, and aircraft to substitute for heavier steel. The trend is especially evident in the automobile industry where significant weight and size reductions were achieved due to material substitutions following the oil shock of the 1970s that led to a major push in the US to conserve energy. The estimated weight of carbon steel used in an average car manufactured in the US declined by 475 pounds between 1978 and 1988. Even though this reduction was a result of substitution by slightly higher quantities of high-strength steel, plastic composites, and aluminum, the average total weight of a US automobile was reduced by over 400 pounds. The cost savings benefited the manufacturers and the consumers, and the environment benefited due to a lower use of fossil fuels. According to the energy guru Amory Lovins, only 1 percent of the energy consumed by a typical internal combustion car moves the driver,[57] the rest moves the material (mostly metal) in which the driver is ensconced. This offers tremendous potential for material reduction (and energy conservation) even in a conventional fossil fuel powered car. As a result, in a radical move, in 2014 Ford Motor Company is planning to release its popular F-150 truck in an aluminum body. This will reduce the weight of the truck by 700 pounds, which will significantly reduce fuel consumption without compromising body strength. Ford expects the cost of producing the vehicle and the price to the consumer to be similar to the current version. The F series from Ford is one of the most profitable vehicle lines in the world and accounts for a third of the company's profits. It is likely that the redesigned product will increase Ford's profitability.[58] In all these cases, the redesigned product may be preferred by consumers not only due to its lower environmental footprint but also its better design that may be lighter or more functional. This contributes to competitive advantage via product differentiation.

Substitution of lighter materials such as aluminum for steel is a positive step but represents incremental innovation. Even while firms are making major strides in material reduction (especially when they are able to identify cost savings), consumers are buying increasing numbers of material-intensive products such as more and larger automobiles. Increasing affluence in developing countries means that more people can afford cars and can buy more than one car. There is also a lower bound on how small products can be made and still be compatible with the physical dimensions and limitations of humans. At the same time, there are limitations on dematerialization due to safety considerations and compliance with regulations for products. While smaller and lighter products lower costs for the firm and for customers, they may also have a negative environmental impact as consumers tend to replace rather than repair, and constantly upgrade to the latest model while throwing perfectly usable older models into landfills, especially in the case of appliances and electronics. Hence, while individual firms can carve out differentiation advantages, the overall impact on the natural environment may be ultimately negative rather than positive.

Miniaturization

Dematerialization also happens as a result of technological advances in miniaturization. For example, silicon wafers have been constantly increasing in size to reduce material losses in cutting out chips from the wafer. IBM uses over 400 acres of silicon wafer material every year at a cost of about $100 million per acre. The increase in total wafer area per year is about 10 to 15 percent.[59] Therefore, less waste not only reduces costs but also reduces environmental impact because the manufacture involves the handling of hazardous chemicals. In this domain, advances in nanotechnology (the manipulation of matter on an atomic and molecular scale) have the potential to generate quantum leaps in the miniaturization of products. This offers opportunities to create new materials and devices with a vast range of applications in medicine, electronics, biomaterials, and energy production. However, each new technology requires careful risk assessment since the positive environmental impacts of nanotechnology may be offset by as yet unknown impacts of toxicity and other environmental impacts of nano-materials.

Nanotechnology offers promising avenues of radical innovation that lead to quantum shifts in dematerialization and new products that may open new industries, consumer uses, and consumer preferences. For example, researchers at HRL Laboratories, the California Institute of Technology, and the University of California at Irvine have created an ultra low-density material, a lattice of hollow tubes of the metal nickel with a volume that is 99.99 percent air. Its density is 0.9 milligrams per cubic centimeter, less than one-thousandth that of water. This metallic micro-lattice can absorb sound, vibration, and shock and can be used for significantly cheaper electrodes for lithium-ion batteries, and lighter-weight materials for automobiles, aircraft, and spacecraft.[60] When this material is commercially manufactured, it has the potential to disrupt or even destroy the steel industry.

Substituting materials with services

In addition to substitution of one product with lower material intensity for a product with a higher material intensity, greater impact can be achieved by substituting a product with a service. Service substitution shifts the mode of consumption from personal ownership of products to provision of services that provide similar functions and promoting significantly lower resource use per unit of consumption.[61]

Such substitution involves selling the function of a product or the service it provides, with the idea that fewer goods will be necessary to meet the same needs. Producing fewer goods leads to fewer environmental impacts in the manufacturing process, and less waste when products outlive their usefulness. For manufacturers and suppliers there is the potential to create more stable profits and improve revenue by selling services, and cutting material and energy costs while maintaining and growing the customer base.

An example is the substitution of telecommuting for transportation. However, this may not necessarily lead to lower environmental impacts in the overall economy if the new product requires investment in substantial material infrastructure (e.g., cellular towers for communications). For the same reason, substitution may not necessarily lead to cost reduction. On the other hand, substitution may change the competitive landscape unless the incumbent firm itself moves into a different industrial space. Some products are better candidates for turning into services than others. Electronic equipment and vehicles, for instance, lend themselves well to a service model (leasing) due to limited life-spans and upfront costs that make them more expensive to purchase outright. For instance, car-sharing organizations offer businesses and individuals car use services that substitute for fleet vehicle or car ownership. When several organizations share the same vehicles, fewer vehicles need to be produced than if all the organizations owned their own. This significantly reduces the need for materials, and reduces the energy and water used, and pollutants emitted during production.

In the early 2000s, Mountain Equipment Co-op, a Canadian outdoor gear retailer, began renting rather than selling outdoor equipment from its stores. This makes outdoor activities affordable to a greater number of people and enables them to try a new sport. Another example is US-based Gage Products Co., a specialty chemical supplier for auto paint shops. Gage moved from solely selling chemical blends for auto painting to providing additional value-added services, helping auto body staff apply the mixtures properly, get through color changes, and reduce the need for solvents. This value-added service eventually attracted larger customers, such as Chrysler, which Gage helped meet new environmental regulatory requirements, reducing pollution through reduced use of chemicals.[62] A well-known example is a change in business model by the carpet company Interface, from selling carpets to leasing carpet tiles, involving the take-back of old carpet tiles and substantially reducing the use of raw fiber to manufacture new carpets. This example will be discussed in more detail in Chapter 4. In the cases described above, the substitution of materials for services not only reduces the environmental footprint but also links consumers more closely to the firm's value chain and hence creates a differentiation competitive advantage for the firm.

Quality improvement

Improvements in quality also generally result in dematerialization. For example, total tire production in the United States has risen over time, following from general increases in both the number of registered vehicles and the total miles of travel. However, the number of tires per million vehicle miles of travel has declined. Such a decline in tire wear can be attributed to improved tire quality, which results directly in a decrease in the quantity of solid waste due to discarded tires. For example, a tire designed to have a service life of 100,000 miles could reduce solid waste from tires by 60 to 75 percent.[63] Other effective tire waste reduction strategies include tire retreading and recycling, as well as the use of discarded tires as vulcanized rubber particles in roadway asphalt mixes. While quality improvements may lead to cost savings due to lower defects and returns, they certainly lead to consumer preferences, higher prices for the product, and hence differentiation competitive advantage.

Energy efficiency

The principles that apply to pollution prevention also apply to energy efficiency. Energy productivity, which measures the output and quality of goods and services per unit of energy input, can be based on either reducing the amount of energy required to produce goods and services, or on increasing the quantity or quality of goods and services produced from the same amount of energy. Savings in energy obviously reduce costs for the firm. As the prices of fossil fuel based energy have risen, this saving has become increasingly substantial, especially for industries such as microprocessor fabrication and aluminum and computer servers that consume huge amounts of energy. Energy savings drop directly to the bottom line of a firm and hence even small reductions in fuel costs have major impacts on the bottom line of industries such as airlines.

Simple solutions such as better and more effective insulation allow buildings to use less heating and cooling energy to achieve and maintain a comfortable temperature. Similarly, better insulation or cladding results in lower transmission losses of heat in steam or water pipelines. The installation of fluorescent or LED lights or natural skylights reduces the amount of energy required to attain the same level of illumination compared to using traditional incandescent light bulbs. Compact fluorescent lights use two-thirds less energy and may last six to ten times longer as compared to incandescent lights. Improvements in energy efficiency are most often achieved by adopting a more efficient technology or production process. In addition to cost savings, lower energy usage also leads to lower emissions and wastes. That is, if a firm burns less fossil fuel, it generates lower greenhouse gases and carbon emissions. According to the International Energy Agency, improved energy efficiency in buildings, industrial processes, and transportation could reduce the world's energy needs in 2050 by one third, and help control global emissions of greenhouse gases.[64]

Amory Lovins, the energy guru and founder of the Rocky Mountain Institute, argues that businesses have abundant opportunities to save 70 to 90 percent of the energy and cost for lighting, fan, and pump systems, 50 percent for electric motors, and 60 percent in areas such as heating, cooling, office equipment, and appliances. In general, up to 75 percent of the electricity used in the US today could be saved with efficiency measures that cost less than the electricity itself.[65]

A report published in 2007 by the McKinsey Global Institute argues that there are sufficient economically viable opportunities for energy productivity improvements that could keep global energy demand growth at less than 1 percent per annum.[66] This is less than half of the 2.2 percent average growth anticipated through 2020 in a business-as-usual scenario. Countries such as Japan have treated energy efficiency as a national security issue for decades because Japan has limited fossil fuel resources and relies heavily on imports. Energy efficiency has enabled it to reduce its level of energy imports from foreign countries.

In addition to cost advantages, there are clear differentiation advantages since customers prefer energy-efficient products and appliances and industries prefer energy-efficient equipment. For example, airlines prefer fuel-efficient planes due to lower operating costs that lead to lower fares and higher profits for airlines.

Cost and differentiation advantage via redesign of products and services

The redesign of a product can not only generate cost savings by reducing material and packaging used, it can also improve consumer value and create preference and price premium in the market. Redesign of products with a focus on reducing their environmental footprint (a process also known as eco-design) has the potential for injecting fresh thinking on product parameters, materials, and specifications that would not otherwise be undertaken during the course of normal product development and improvement processes. Such fresh thinking has the potential for unconventional or out-of-the-box innovations in product design that would not normally happen if environmental and social impacts were not considered.[67]

At the simplest level, an example is Apple's products and packaging. Apple's design and engineering managers incorporated environmental impacts into their product design process and developed product packaging that was attractive for the consumer but was also slim and light and yet protected the product. In the process, they reduced materials used, the waste generated in production, and the emissions produced during transportation. For example, the packaging for iPhone 4 was 42 percent less than for the original iPhone. As a result, 80 percent more iPhone 4 boxes fit on each shipping pallet, more pallets fit on each boat and plane, and fewer boats and planes were used, resulting in lower CO_2 emissions.[68] This trend has continued with subsequent product launches such as the iPhone 5 and the iPad Air.

Another company that has a well-developed product life-cycle analysis for assessing and reducing environmental impact is Procter & Gamble (P&G). P&G helped pioneer product life-cycle analysis to determine a product's environmental footprint, from the procurement of raw materials to the product's use by consumers and its ultimate disposal. In the case of its laundry detergents, the life-cycle assessment revealed that the heating of water in the washing machine consumed the highest amount of energy. P&G focused its efforts in this area, first with its Ariel product in Western Europe and then with Tide in North America, introducing products that performed well in cold water. Ariel Excel Gel was designed from scratch for high-performance cleaning at low temperatures to bring about reductions in environmental impact, expending less energy, water, packaging, and waste. This has led to higher market share in Europe and a clear consumer preference for P&G's detergents. Further, by replacing cardboard shipping boxes on Ariel with seal-tight plastic bags, P&G in Turkey found a way to use significantly less material while delivering the product to market. Entirely recyclable, these bags consumed 80 percent less packaging material than boxes, took up 20 percent less space during transport and storage, and helped speed up the packaging line. This packaging was subsequently adopted by the company worldwide. This packaging not only saves costs but, for P&G's retail customers, the new transparent film outer covering allows for easier stock management with faster recognition of brands and sizes.

Because the packaging can be opened without tools, it is easier to handle. It also maximizes shelf space for retailers, helping reduce out-of-stock situations.[69]

In building design and construction, designers use eco-design from the choice of materials to the type of energy that is being consumed and the disposal of waste. Local raw materials are less costly and reduce the financial and environmental costs of shipping, fuel consumption, and CO_2 emissions. Certified green building materials such as wood from sustainably managed forest plantations, with accreditations from companies such as the Forest Stewardship Council (FSC) or the Pan-European Forest Certification Council (PEFCC) often create strong consumer preference and price premiums. Recyclable and recycled materials are also used in construction. Materials that have been reclaimed, such as wood from a demolished building or from a junkyard, can be given a second life by re-using them as support beams in a new building or in the manufacture of furniture. Stones from an excavation can be used in a retaining wall. The re-use of these items means that less energy is consumed in making new products and a new natural aesthetic quality is achieved. Eco-design of buildings adds both environmental value and consumer value to buildings. New designs in buildings can also use water recycling from gray water, and renewable energy generated from solar, wind, or geothermal sources. Buildings that integrate passive energy systems heat buildings using non-mechanical methods, thereby optimizing natural resources. The use of optimal daylight plays an integral role in passive energy systems. This involves the positioning and location of a building to allow and make use of the sunlight throughout the year. By using natural sunlight, thermal mass is stored into the building materials such as concrete and can generate enough warmth for room heating. Green roofs partially or completely cover roofs with plants or other vegetation. The covered roof creates insulation that helps regulate the outside temperature. It also retains water, providing a water recycling system and provides soundproofing, ideal for noisy areas. Buildings with these eco-design features are highly preferred by residential and industrial customers seeking the coveted LEED (Leadership in Energy and Environmental Design) certification.

With increasing awareness, customers are demanding transparency about a product or service's sustainability impacts and thus firms can generate differentiation preferences (and also cost advantages) in almost any industry by paying attention to these features in design.

Cost advantage via industrial symbiosis

Industrial symbiosis brings elements of waste reduction, dematerialization, recycling, and energy efficiency together to generate cost savings and extra revenues. Industrial symbiosis involves the sharing of services, utilities, and by-products between different facilities in order to add value, reduce costs, and improve the environment.[70] It is a closed-loop system between different industrial units where the wastes of one unit become the input for another unit (compared to a closed-loop system within a single firm where it re-uses its wastes as inputs).

An often-cited case of industrial symbiosis is the waste exchange network in the small industrial city of Kalundborg in Denmark, seventy-five miles from Copenhagen. The main facilities in this systems are: Asnæs, Denmark's largest coal-fired power station with a 1,500 megawatts capacity; Statoil, Denmark's largest oil refinery with a capacity of 4.8 million tons; Gyproc, which makes 14 million square meters of gypsum wallboard annually; Novo Nordisk, an international biotechnological company that produces 40 percent of the world's supply of insulin and industrial enzymes at the plant; and the City of Kalundborg that supplies heating to the 20,000 residents and water to homes and industries.

This network evolved without any initial planning, as a series of bilateral deals that identified uses for waste of each pair of participants. In the early 1970s, Gyproc located its facility in Kalundborg to take advantage of the fuel gas available from Statoil, which was being flared off as waste. At that time, similar to most fossil fuel power stations, the coal-fired Asnæs power station operated at 40 percent thermal efficiency, with the majority of energy generated being wasted from the smokestack. Asnæs began to supply the city with steam for its new district heating system in 1981 and then added Novo Nordisk and Statoil as customers for steam. The district heating replaced about 3,500 oil furnaces, a significant source of air pollution. The power plant uses salt water, from the fjord, for some of its cooling needs. By doing so, it reduces the withdrawals of fresh water from a local lake. The resulting by-product is hot salt water, some of which is supplied to the fish farm's ponds. In 1992, the power plant began substituting fuels by using surplus refinery gas in place of some coal. This happened after Statoil built a sulfur recovery unit to comply with regulations on sulfur emissions. Over a million tons of sludge from Novo Nordisk's processes and from the fish farm's water treatment plant is used as fertilizer on nearby farms. A cement company uses the power plant's desulfurized fly ash. Asnæs reacts the sulfur dioxide in its stack gas with calcium carbonate, thereby making calcium sulfate (gypsum), which it sells to Gyproc, supplying two-thirds of the latter firm's needs. The refinery's desulfurization operation produces pure liquid sulfur, which is trucked to Kemira, a sulfuric acid producer. Surplus yeast from insulin production at Novo Nordisk goes to farmers as pig food. This web of recycling and re-use has generated revenues and cost savings for the companies involved and has significantly reduced pollution.[71] Each waste exchange was undertaken bilaterally by two players based on the potential to generate financial savings and has at the same time led to significant positive environmental impacts.

In spite of the tremendous potential of industrial symbiosis or industrial ecology to reduce environmental impact and generate costs savings, very little progress has been made since the Kalundborg symbiosis emerged in the 1970s. Canada has initiated a few such exchanges. At Burnside Park in Halifax, Nova Scotia, supported by Dalhousie University's Eco-Efficiency Centre, more than 1,500 businesses have been improving their environmental performance and developing profitable partnerships. There are two greenfield industrial parks in Alberta: TaigaNova Eco-Industrial Park in Atha-basca oil sands and Innovista Eco-Industrial Park in the foothills of the Rocky Mountains west of Edmonton. This is an area of potential development for industrial zones all over the world.

Differentiation and cost advantage via improved reputation and license to operate

Stakeholders such as local communities and NGOs may protest and express concerns about the negative environmental and social impacts of a firm's operations. Such protests attract the attention of the media and other stakeholders, resulting in consumers boycotting the firm's products and services. Media reports, and wide communication via the Internet, spread information about the protests and the environmental and social impacts to a large number of stakeholder groups across the world and thereby influence the firm's reputation. A negative reputation could result in lost sales, lower stock prices, and diminished access to new markets.

Stakeholders including shareholders, consumers, NGOs, and governments increasingly demand greater transparency and accountability from a firm regarding the social and environmental impacts in its value chain. Starting with the SuperFund legislation in the US, governments were mandated to hold any firm liable for toxic contamination even if they had only transported or stored or handled a chemical and had not actually manufactured it.[72] Similarly, as in the example of Nike described in Chapter 2, there are numerous instances of consumers and NGOs holding firms accountable for social equity and environmental impacts for products manufactured directly or indirectly by them. These impacts include working conditions in sweatshops, whether or not the workers earn a living wage, whether farmers are being paid fair prices for commodities, whether habitats and rainforests are destroyed as a result of intensive cultivation of coffee and other crops, whether there is depletion of soil and groundwater due to intensive cultivation of cotton, and so on. At the same time, firms are being held accountable for environmental impacts during the consumption of the product or service. The issues relate to energy and water use during consumption and the biodegradability and toxicity of products that affect safe disposal. These risks cannot be passed up or down the value chain to suppliers and customers any more and firms have to ultimately assume responsibility for their products and services from cradle to grave. Another risk that most firms now face is the vulnerability of their ever-more complex global supply chains to increasingly unpredictable climate change events such as tsunamis, hurricanes, and storms. Insurance companies such as Swiss Re and Munich Re have invested resources in modeling climate change since the early 1990s since their business viability depends upon being able to predict potential liabilities related to extreme weather events. Shareholder activism over environmental and social impacts of publicly listed firms has been steadily increasing in recent years.[73]

In an interconnected world, it is very difficult, or almost impossible, for firms to isolate or hide environmental and social impacts in their global supply chains. A negative or positive incident spreads almost instantly via the Internet to stakeholders all across the world[74] and consequently larger numbers of customers increasingly demand complete transparency. If the firm attempts to hide any information about negative sustainability impacts, customers are informed straight away through a variety of sources. The information on the Internet and in the media that customers are influenced by may or may not be accurate and may be biased, subjective, and opinionated. Therefore, it is in the firm's best interests to be transparent and open. In 1989, against strong advice from its public relations advisers, Norsk Hydro released one of the world's first audited corporate environmental reports that showed the extent of its emissions and negative environmental impacts. Unexpectedly, instead of condemnation, the company attracted a great deal of praise and support from all its stakeholders including customers.[75] This also set the standard for other firms to follow.

Reputation and brand equity loss for a company are translated into loss of current and potential sales and also affects the firm's current and future operations and legitimacy. Taking the example of Shell, the company became proactive after it suffered significant losses to its image after the hanging of author Ken Saro-Wiwa, the leader of the Ogoni people in Nigeria. Saro-Wiwa led a nonviolent campaign against environmental degradation of the land and waters of Ogoniland due to the extraction of crude oil by oil companies, especially Royal Dutch Shell. The Nigerian military government arrested Saro-Wiwa in 1995, hastily tried him before a special military tribunal, and hanged him on charges viewed as politically motivated and completely unfounded. His execution provoked international outrage and resulted in Nigeria's suspension from the Commonwealth of Nations for over three years and a series of cases that held Shell accountable for alleged human rights violations in Nigeria, including summary execution, crimes against humanity, torture, inhumane treatment, and arbitrary arrest and detention.[76] During the same year, in 1995, Shell became locked into a widely publicized international conflict with Greenpeace and many other stakeholders over the disposal of the *Brent Spar* offshore platform in the North Sea.[77] In order to avoid further damage to its reputation and brand, Shell took a proactive stance in its sustainability practices and in transparency with stakeholders after these incidents.

BP's *Deepwater Horizon* oil rig environmental disaster in 2010 led to the company's brand name falling off the list of the world's top 100 most valuable brands according to Interbrand, the world's leading brand valuation company.[78] The valuation of any brand is based on expected future sales and earnings; environmental disasters lead to a decline in the number of customers willing to deal with the company and buy its products. In previous decades, oil companies Exxon and Shell were negatively affected by the *Exxon Valdez* accident in Prince William Sound in 1989 and Shell's *Brent Spar* oil rig disposal conflict with Greenpeace in the North Sea in 1995, respectively. And in the clothing and footwear industry, Nike's valuation suffered when it was criticized for working conditions in its contractors' sweatshops during the 1990s; there was criticism in 2006 over working conditions in Honduran sweatshops manufacturing products for Martha Stewart Living; and similarly for several major clothing brands after over a thousand deaths due to the collapse of subcontractors' facilities in Bangladesh in 2013. Food giant Monsanto suffered serious adverse publicity after the controversy over its genetically modified seeds during the late 1990s.

In 2012, after several years of concerns being expressed by some NGOs over poor working conditions at Apple's contractors' facilities in China, Apple finally granted access to an NGO, the Fair Labor Association (FLA), to conduct special voluntary audits of several facilities, including factories owned by Foxconn, the world's largest electronics manufacturer, in Shenzen and Chengdu. Apple's problems with the Taiwanese company Foxconn, which manufactures almost all of its devices, started in 2010 when several workers committed suicide at a plant in Longhua, China. This plant employs between 300,000 and 400,000 workers. Apple CEO Tim Cook chose to make his first overseas visit to China to demonstrate that he took these concerns seriously and to avoid jeopardizing Apple's sales and share price.[79]

Commenting on the prosecution of Wal-Mart under the Foreign Corrupt Practices Act in the US over its bribery scandal in Mexico, Goldman Sachs estimates that such violations typically undervalue the stock for at least three years and reduce profits by around 9 percent. This would mean at least $6.5 billion in lost profits to Wal-Mart, an amount that is huge in comparison to the amount of bribes paid by it.[80] Similarly, it was pointed out above that BP's investors lost 54 percent of their stock value after the *Deepwater Horizon* oil spill.

In all these cases, while sales may eventually recover after a few years, the decline in sales, brand equity, and shareholder equity for a period of time has negative consequences for several stakeholders of the firm. Some customers are permanently driven away to other providers and never buy the firm's products again. In addition to lost sales, it is difficult to estimate the value of the discounts that the firm has to offer in order to attract more price-conscious customers and the loss borne by investors for a period of time.

Even shareholders are increasingly savvy and concerned about potential risks, liabilities, and reputation issues related to unsustainable practices. Between 1998 and 2003, Talisman Energy, a Canadian oil company, suffered from stock price under-performance. This confounded analysts who ran only the financial numbers. However, shareholders discounted the price of the firm significantly lower than its current and past financial performance. The market was obviously taking into consideration the international outcry and NGO protests over the firm's operations in Darfur. It was perceived that Talisman was indirectly supporting and financing genocide in Southern Sudan by supporting the brutal Sudanese regime via the large oil royalties it paid to the government. Only after Talisman sold its operations in Sudan in 2003 did its stock price begin to climb.[81] These are but illustrative examples among the many such cases of impact on reputations of companies worldwide.

License to operate

Many firms have directly experienced the reputation risks of negative social and environmental impacts. As described above, firms have lost considerable sales and brand equity, and shareholders have lost significant wealth, over environmental accidents or negative social impacts. They have also realized that a negative reputation affects their license to operate within communities and markets. Consequently, many firms have traditionally undertaken philanthropic, citizenship, and community relationship activities in order to maintain a license to operate within their communities. However, increasingly, firms have realized that they are under a great deal of scrutiny by several stakeholders and the best way to enhance license to operate is via genuine actions rather than via public relations that may be viewed as greenwashing. For example, when S.C. Johnson Co. reformulated its products to reduce or eliminate environmentally toxic and harmful ingredients and advertised them as green and marketed them under its own home-grown label Greenlist, there was a backlash and lawsuits from consumers in 2008 and 2009 because felt that the company was misrepresenting the label as an external third-party certification.[82] While corporate profits may bounce back after a period of time, the lost value during the negative reputation period, and the lost opportunities when the license to operate is constrained, are never regained.

Some countries in Western Europe are establishing increasingly stringent standards for social and environmental performance by firms wanting to conduct business in their markets. In 2011, the European Union announced that it would require all air carriers that fly into the EU to offset their carbon emissions. All flights arriving at, or departing from, EU airports are subject to the EU Emissions Trading Scheme, which requires that airlines purchase enough carbon offsets to compensate for the amount of carbon dioxide they generate on these routes. A carbon offset usually takes the form of financial support for projects that reduce greenhouse gas emissions, such as wind farms, forestry projects or the destruction of pollutants. If an airline fails to purchase sufficient carbon offsets, it will have to pay penalties and make up the shortfall during the following year. Several countries, including the US, contend that this requirement violates the international Open Skies Agreement, through which nations grant each other access to their airspace to promote free trade. In 2012, the EU Court of Justice dismissed this complaint.[83] Last November, the European Commission suspended the carbon emissions laws on flights taking off or landing from EU member states after the International Civil Aviation Organization (ICAO) agreed to work toward a *global* plan to cut airline emissions. The EU stopped the clock for one year regarding aviation's inclusion within the EU Emissions Trading Scheme until after the ICAO General Assembly in 2013.[84] In 2014, as a stop-gap measure, the EU has agreed that foreign airlines will be liable for offsetting their emissions for the portion of their journey that takes place over EU airspace and not the entire journey, that is, a JAL flight from Tokyo will be liable only when it enters the EU airspace. While regulations may be delayed, they are inevitable and proactive firms are preparing to develop technologies and capabilities to reap competitive advantage rather than disadvantage in this scenario.

Faster approvals

A firm's license to operate and its reputation for sustainability practices translate into faster project approvals, which in turn lead to lower costs and first or early mover advantages. In many global jurisdictions, especially in developed countries, new projects require open processes of environmental and public review. The process invites input from various stakeholders including communities and NGOs. These processes are much more contentious when they involve exploitation of natural resources or are located in environmentally sensitive habitats or indigenous communities. However, even new retail locations, such as new Wal-Mart stores, attract contentious review processes because they are perceived to negatively affect small businesses and local communities. Delays in implementing projects result in lost sales and profits for the firm. At the same time, these projects incur costs and embedded investments during the review process. The investments incur interest charges and do not pay back until the project comes on stream and begins to generate production and sales.

During the early 1990s, Amoco Canada Petroleum Ltd. (now owned by BP) underwent several years of a long process of environmental review in the environmentally sensitive Whaleback region of Alberta, 80 miles from Calgary. The mounting pressure from various stakeholders during the review process prompted the Alberta Energy Conservation Board (ERCB) to reject a project for the first time in its sixty-year history. Amoco was shocked by the unprecedented ruling that denied it permission to start exploration and drilling. The anticipated natural gas reservoir in this location was around 1.2 trillion cubic feet. The ERCB subsequently granted permission to other firms with more proactive and positive environmental performance records with strategies to use more responsible environmental practices to explore and drill in the Whaleback. Thus Amoco suffered significant costs during the review process and a loss of revenues and profits that failed to materialize.

Access to new markets

Reputation and license to operate are important not only in existing markets but also for new market access. Projects funded by some governments, by the World Bank, the International Finance Corporation, and the European Union require the firms to have a track record of proactive sustainability practices and capabilities to achieve positive environmental and social performance indicators as outcomes of these projects. These requirements are continuously escalating and becoming more stringent, forcing firms to acquire capabilities and expertise in assessing the environmental and social impacts of projects and developing sustainable strategies to achieve positive social and environmental impacts.

As developing countries such as China wake up to the realities of their degrading environments and escalating disparities in income and social equity, they are becoming increasingly concerned about more sustainable models of growth and economic development. There are opportunities for firms to offer business models that leapfrog traditional smokestack polluting technologies and move to mobile communication platforms instead of landline-based communication platforms, renewable or hydrogen-based fuels instead of internal combustion technologies based on fossil fuels, distributed generation of renewable power instead of large-scale centralized fossil fuel based power plants, and so on. Firms with sustainable business models and technologies will have a future advantage in entering and being successful in such markets.

The development of sustainable technologies, products, services, and business models is also driven by changing consumer preferences.

Consumers are increasingly concerned about the cradle-to-grave (value chain) social and environmental footprints of the products and services they consume. They are generally not willing to pay premiums for sustainable products and services but nevertheless prefer those with lower social and environmental footprints. In some government jurisdictions, and in the procurement policies of some corporations such as Wal-Mart (discussed in Chapter 2), environmental features (such as recycled content) are mandated. Firms without a portfolio of investments in sustainable technologies, products, services, and/or business models risk future market disadvantage.

Example: Wal-Mart's move to organic cotton

Wal-Mart's move into T-shirts made out of organic cotton is an illustration of how their strategy reduces the risks of an unsustainable business while generating avenues of competitive advantage for Wal-Mart. The main environmental criticism against the cotton industry is that the growing of cotton uses more pesticides and synthetic fertilizers than almost any other crop. In 2004, a buyer for Sam's Club ordered organic cotton yoga outfits. They were a big success and as Wal-Mart was developing its sustainability strategy, they realized that organic products mattered to its working-class and middle-class consumers and could be a source of competitive advantage. Wal-Mart began working with a nonprofit trade group called the Organic Exchange, which has been promoting the use of organic cotton around the world since 2002. As a part of the process, Wal-Mart sent its executives to organic cotton farms in Texas, California, and Turkey, the world's biggest grower of organic cotton. The field immersion experience was most valuable in the executives' learning about the health impacts of pesticides and fertilizers. Today, Wal-Mart is one of the world's biggest buyers of organic cotton and sellers of organic cotton products including clothing, bed-sheets, and towels. While Patagonia converted its entire sportswear line to organic ten years ago, Wal-Mart's massive buying clout and consumer influence was a game changer for organic farmers, who now had an assured market for their production.

While Wal-Mart is constantly under attack by social and environmental NGOs for one or more of its practices or operational impacts, the move to organic cotton helped it manage some of the NGO criticism and address some of its operational impacts. Instead of dealing only with its suppliers, Wal-Mart's executives chose to work directly with farmers in California and Turkey and thus fostered deep stakeholder engagement and an understanding and appreciation of the impacts of pesticides and fertilizers. This allowed some NGOs such as Organic Exchange to work with Wal-Mart to help it implement the practice. Reputation enhancement is a gradual process based on consistency of actions and practices of a firm and this practice has set Wal-Mart on the road toward overcoming negative criticisms and improving its image among its employees and external stakeholders. The practice established strong and loyal supply chain linkages with farmers of organic cotton and increased customer loyalty. In selling low-cost generic clothes, linen, and toweling, Wal-Mart was able to generate competitive advantage through product differentiation for the same colors, quality, and price. Even though smaller players such as Patagonia have been selling apparel made out of organic cotton for over a decade, Wal-Mart gained first-mover advantage among large department stores and changed the competitive playing field.

Competitive advantage via radical and disruptive innovation

Perhaps the most exciting potential benefit for businesses as a result of integrating sustainability thinking into corporate decision-making processes is the potential for radical innovation and disruptive new technologies, products, services, and business models that could lead to competitive advantage, whether via cost or differentiation advantage, in existing and new markets.[85] Earlier in this chapter, some examples were provided of simple waste reduction and energy efficiency solutions that streamlined operations, improved efficiencies, and reduced costs. In this section, the focus is on radical new clean technologies and business models.

Lacking internal knowledge on how to manage social and environmental impacts of its operations, firms seek input from various stakeholders such as NGOs, customers, suppliers, local communities, governments, etc. These interactions open up the firms to new perspectives, and potentially radical new thinking about products, processes, and business models could emerge.[86] The move from conventional to sustainable products and services is a discontinuity in the innovation trajectory of a firm and has the potential to lead to a change in its technological paradigm. This could possibly lead to the emergence of a new industry or the creative destruction of an existing industry. Firms that are more flexible to pursue new opportunities without the liabilities of existing or legacy assets can reap substantial competitive advantage.

Societal concern for sustainability, as a major change in the business environment, has sparked innovation in clean technologies, cleaner production processes, use of renewable materials, and innovative new business models to alleviate poverty and protect ecosystems. The current clean technology landscape is diverse and bubbling with innovations in agricultural biotechnology, energy efficiency, power storage, transportation, clean water, renewable materials, waste elimination, and reduction of air and carbon emissions. Many firms are investing in these technologies, products and services, and business models in order to build future sources of competitive advantage. Societal concerns about climate change have resulted in an escalation in the development of continuously lower cost and more efficient photovoltaic technologies and wind turbines. Firms in China have recently become leaders in low-cost renewable energy technologies such as solar panels and water heating systems. During the last decade, automobile companies have invested substantially in cleaner fuels, efficient diesel engines, hybrid and electric vehicles, and fuel cell technologies, each hoping that their technology will emerge as the competitive leader. Advances in materials science, biotechnology, nanotechnology, engineering, design, and business models are driving environmentally sustainable innovation inexorably forward.

Low environmental impact services are replacing high-impact physical products, for example, in telecommuting versus transportation (web conferences versus flying across the world). Renewable energy is developing rapidly and reaching cost parity with conventional fossil fuels. Fuel cell and alternate propulsion technologies are at various stages of commercialization to replace the internal combustion engine. Distributed energy and communication are replacing gigantic centralized power plants and telecommunication centers. Micro-lending is benefiting millions of poor people every day as compared to smaller numbers of corporations and affluent clients served by large corporate banks. Such innovations will be discussed in more detail in the following chapters.

Some of these new technologies are displacing existing technologies and the products and business models that are based on these technologies. This trend has been gathering momentum over the last decade. Evolving technologies also have the potential to disrupt entire industries and render existing investments in capabilities and assets valueless. For example, the rapid evolution of digital imaging technologies and convergence of technologies from different industries into mobile devices has destroyed industries such as the photo film and their business models based on film processing (Kodak) and product categories such as the electronic organizer (dominated during the 1990s by the Palm Pilot). Such disruption has meant that the competitive landscape of major players in industries such as digital cameras and telecommunications has changed dramatically. Witness the recent bankruptcy of Kodak in 2012. Just a decade ago Kodak was a profitable and successful photo imaging company. While a great deal of this innovation was not driven by sustainable objectives, digitization and nanotechnology have the potential to reduce material use and waste, and generate positive environmental and social impacts.

Of course, in this emerging field of technological innovation, competitive advantage will be reaped by only a few. A major change in the technological paradigm in an industry is usually characterized by a large number of new entrants experimenting with new product designs. A dominant design emerges after industry consolidation and a large number of exits. Emerging clean technology industries are currently at different stages of development. For example, while the solar photovoltaic industry has been characterized by a high degree of experimentation and new entries since 2003, the wind turbine manufacturing industry is more mature and began to move toward consolidation as far back as 2002–04 with acquisitions by large incumbent players such as GE and Siemens, and mergers of pioneering firms such as Vestas and NEG Micon.

Radical new business models and products are also emerging as firms enter new and unfamiliar contexts such as the base of the income pyramid markets, where people have substantial unmet needs and the income levels are extremely low—often between one and three dollars a day—to develop innovative new business models that deliver shareholder value while building economic capacity and micro-entrepreneurship among the marginalized poor. These models are intended to be socially equitable and help preserve the environment. Engagement in the base of the pyramid, a market that is radically different from higher-income and middle-income markets, is leading to reverse innovations such as GE's hand-held imaging scanner (the Vscan) that costs a fraction of larger machines.

While these new technologies and business models are proliferating, their effective commercialization for extraction of economic value requires patient capital, learning, and the development of organizational capabilities. Therefore, firms that are behind the curve in this area will either be at a disadvantage in the future competitive landscape or have to leapfrog by acquiring companies with successful clean technology applications and/or sustainable business models.

Summary

Firms that ignore societal demands for addressing the negative social and environmental impacts of their operations along their entire value chains are vulnerable to escalating business risks that could affect short-term and long-term economic performance. Short-term risks include civil and criminal liability and loss of license to operate and negative impacts on reputation, which translate into lower sales and shareholder value. Long-term risks include risk to resource base (and inputs), changing customer preferences, access to markets, and loss of competitive advantage to radical and disruptive new technologies. In addition, increasingly unpredictable climate change events such as tsunamis, hurricanes, and storms affect the stability of their global supply chains. Firms that adopt a sustainable strategy not only manage the risks discussed in this chapter but also have the potential to realize short-term and long-term competitive benefits.

Ignoring the risks of an unsustainable strategy has the potential to jeopardize shareholder value generation both in the short term and in the long term. Averting these risks and adopting a sustainable strategy has the potential for generating competitive advantage for a firm via cost savings through reduction and prevention of wastes, lower material and energy use, lower costs of regulatory compliance, faster approvals and lower project costs, lower legal costs, and lower insurance premiums; and via differentiation that creates consumer preference and price premiums through product, process, and business model redesign, improved reputation and brand equity, access to new markets, and radical and disruptive innovation. A clear understanding of the competitive advantages that can be generated by a sustainable strategy helps a firm develop business logic for beginning its transformation to a sustainable organization. Table 3.1 summarizes the link between sustainability strategy and competitive advantage.

Table 3.1 **Sustainability strategy and competitive advantage**

Sustainability strategy	Risks	Competitive advantage
Pollution control	Reduced legal risk No shield against risk of accidents, emergent regulations, civil liabilities	*Cost disadvantage* Investments do not pay back
Pollution prevention	Reduced risks of: Accidents Civil & criminal liabilities Disruption of operations Loss of sales Reduction of brand equity/shareholder value	*Cost advantages* Greater license to operate Reduced capital investment Higher yields/productivity Lower costs of waste disposal Lower material/energy use Lower insurance costs Revenues from by-products *Differentiation* Improved reputation License to operate
Eco-efficiency: Dematerialization Recycling/reuse Process/product redesign Product life cycle analysis Miniaturization Substitution of material with service Quality improvement	Reduced risks of: Increasing material/energy prices as resources get scarce Obsolete/uncompetitive products & technologies	*Cost advantage* Lower material/energy costs *Differentiation* Environmental certification Improved product quality Improved product design Lower consumer use cost Innovations in products & business models Improved reputation/license to operate

➡

Sustainability strategy	Risks	Competitive advantage
Industrial symbiosis	Reduced risks of: Regulations, accidents, liabilities & disruption of operations by stakeholders	*Cost advantages* Revenues from wastes; reduced cost of inputs/energy (wastes from other businesses) *Differentiation* Improved reputation/license to operate Faster project approvals: early mover
Fair trade, fair prices, human rights, working conditions in global Supply chains	Reduced risks of: Disruption of operations Loss of sales Reduction in shareholder value/brand equity	*Differentiation* Improved reputation/license to operate Greater access to existing & new markets Faster project approvals/lower project costs/early mover
Transparency	Reduced risk of backlash from consumers/NGOs related to greenwashing	*Differentiation* Greater access to existing and new markets Improved reputation/license to operate Faster project approvals: early mover
Radical/disruptive innovation		Competitive imagination Disruption of industries Future long-term competitive advantage

This chapter has explained the linkages between corporate practices and strategies to address a firm's sustainability impacts and competitive advantage in the form of lower costs, differentiation of products and services, and radical innovations that lead to the creative destruction of industries. The following chapters address how to implement a sustainable strategy by building logic, changing mindsets, and developing capabilities.

Four
Building logic: Core business proposition and sustainable value

The greatest danger in times of turbulence is not the turbulence; it is to act with yesterday's logic.

Peter F. Drucker, *management thinker*

We can't solve problems by using the same kind of thinking we used when we created them.

Albert Einstein, *physicist*

Societal demands that business address sustainability challenges and deliver social and environmental performance in addition to economic performance have escalated during the last decade. Achieving triple bottom-line performance by firms requires the incorporation of social and environmental metrics in their operations, strategies, products, processes, and business models. Corporate strategy is further complicated because societal understanding of sustainability challenges and the role of business in addressing them is evolving. For example, during the 1970s, societal demands focused on requiring firms to clean up visible pollution and toxic emissions; during the

1980s, the focus turned to the elimination of CFC emissions to halt damage to the Earth's ozone layer; and during the 1990s, the focus was on reducing greenhouse gas emissions to address climate change and global warming. In terms of social impacts, during this period, societal expectations for corporate social performance changed from philanthropy, to job creation, to worker safety, to employee welfare and development, to community development. Each phase required firms to develop increasingly complex strategies and practices. During the 2000s, the societal expectations have evolved to even more complex social and environmental performance metrics: the reduction or elimination of the carbon footprint in complex global value chains, while reducing poverty and promoting social justice, fair trade, fair wages, and humane working conditions.

The evolving expectations and succession of changes in the environment of business create volatility, uncertainty, complexity, and ambiguity (VUCA[87]) for the firm. In order to position their firm for competitive advantage when major changes take place in the business environment, managers need a grounded understanding of the current logic of their business model so that they can change and adapt this logic to identify opportunities in a sustainable world and innovate to capitalize on these opportunities. The business logic includes:

- An understanding of the core business proposition in terms of the customer needs that the business meets and the customer utility that is delivered by the firm's products and services

- The unique capabilities that enable the firm to meet the need and deliver the utility

- How delivering the same consumer utility via sustainable products, services, and business model creates sustainable value by generating corporate value and competitive advantage

While Chapter 6 discusses, in-depth, the critical capabilities that firms need in order to innovate successfully for a sustainable world, this chapter focuses on understanding the core business proposition and sustainable value.

An understanding of the business logic provides a frame of reference within which managers can develop a long-term strategy that integrates sustainable practices and generates sustainable innovations instead of unproductively and continually reacting and responding to each and every change in environmental and social regulation or societal concern, demand, and trend. The transformation process is depicted in Figure 4.1.

Figure 4.1 **Core business proposition and sustainable value**

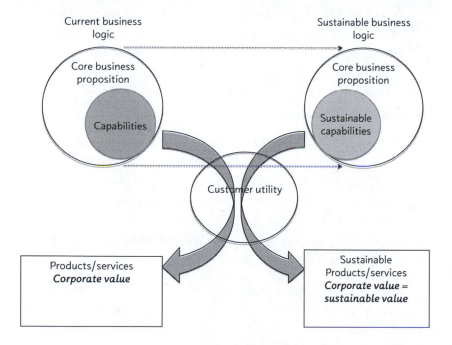

For example, managers of a firm that faces the challenge of building a strategy for reducing its carbon footprint may develop the strategy under alternate business logics:

1. The logic of compliance with regulations while pursuing the current business model. This logic focuses on maintaining the current core fossil fuel based business model intact and focusing on costly investments in pollution and emissions control

equipment to reduce GHGs. This firm would be likely to lobby against regulations for pollution control because responding to regulations affects its competitiveness negatively

2. **The logic of cost reduction while pursuing the current business model.** This strategy focuses on adapting the current business model via eco-efficiency and investments in incremental innovations to reduce carbon emissions at source by making the manufacturing and operating processes more efficient and products lighter and less material-intensive. As described in Chapter 3, this would also generate significant costs savings via reduction in materials, waste, and energy. However, this would not require a change in the current business model and the firm cannot achieve a zero carbon footprint but rather can substantially reduce its footprint in a cost-effective manner

3. **The logic of the carbon footprint as a business opportunity.** This logic views carbon constraints as a potential source of competitive advantage and investing in radical innovations in business models based on clean technologies. Not only would these business models generate carbon credits that could realize revenues as carbon constraints and markets grow, but they also lead to new products and markets

The business logic driving responses to social and environmental issues would determine both *when* (as an early mover or as a follower) and *how* (types of strategy and practices) the firm moves from reducing the negative costs of carbon, to reducing its carbon footprint, to becoming carbon neutral, to achieving competitive advantage in a carbon-constrained world.

In order to develop sustainable business logic, managers need to:

1. Focus on the sustainability issues that are the most relevant for their current and future business (Chapter 2)

2. Understand how their sustainability strategy connects to their core business proposition

3. Realize how focusing on the core business proposition can lead to sustainable business models, products, and services that simultaneously create corporate value and current and future competitive advantage

4. Know which existing capabilities of the firm can be leveraged to develop the sustainability strategy and which capabilities need to be developed and/or enhanced

While the leveraging and development of capabilities is discussed in Chapter 6, this chapter focuses on helping managers understand the link between their core business proposition and sustainable strategy.

Core business proposition: Connecting sustainability to customer utility

Not only can a firm significantly reduce its sustainability footprint by developing business models that substitute services for materials[88] or address unmet needs in the base of the pyramid markets, but it can potentially simultaneously generate competitive advantage. However, this requires innovations in products, services, and business models. Such innovations are normally difficult even when they are routine and incremental because managers find it difficult to balance their focus on their current job goals and responsibilities with creative thinking about the future. Managers busy with everyday routines and responsibilities usually find it difficult to think beyond the current technologies used in their operations, and their products, services, and markets. For example, in Chapter 3, examples of solid waste reduction in the plastics division of DuPont and in the Canadian oil industry were presented. Initially, managers in these companies actively resisted further solid waste reduction because they perceived that the waste percentages were within acceptable industry norms.

Therefore, it is important to change the context and paradigm within which managers innovate by helping them change their focus from the product or service to the unique value or solution that their firm provides to the consumer or the utility that the consumer derives from their product or service. Managers usually have a good understanding of their current customers and their current markets and it is often a stretch for them to think about completely new markets with new customer preferences and profiles. It is easier for managers to innovate incrementally in order to deliver similar value and utility to their customers with a lower material impact while creating positive environmental and social benefits. However, once begun, this process of incremental innovation could spark a visualization of the next steps in expanding the customer base and entering new markets with radical and even disruptive products and business models that significantly enhance a firm's sustainability performance.

During day-to-day operations, managers usually are forced to focus on the products and services they sell instead of on the utility or solutions that their products deliver to their customers. To use an overly simplistic example, customers are really interested in the holes that are produced by the drills that they buy rather than in the drills themselves. Manufacturers of power tools such as Black & Decker can continue to innovate more sophisticated, powerful, and expensive power drills but if another product comes along that makes holes better, more cheaply, and more quickly than the power drills, the firm can lose its market overnight. Moreover, if a firm innovates a solution to meet a customer need that does not require drilling a hole (for example, joining two surfaces with a very strong adhesive strip instead of a fastener), the drill manufacturer will be disrupted out of business.

As briefly outlined in Chapter 3, this argument is illustrated by what happened to Kodak, a powerhouse in photographic film manufacture and processing. Kodak filed for bankruptcy in 2012 and now only has a few thousand employees versus the 65,000 it had in the late 1990s. Kodak's capabilities lay in manufacturing high-quality photographic film at reasonable cost and generating profits from this film and the photographic paper used by its vast network of photo processing machines installed in retail stores—mainly drugstores and pharmacies—across the world. However, with the advent of digital technology, Kodak's managers remained fixated on their products and appeared unable to understand, or chose to ignore, that their customers' needs were increasingly now met by digital photographs. They remained focused on their own product (film and paper), capabilities (manufacture of film and paper and processing machines), and business model (network of film processors) rather than their customers' needs and the *utility* delivered, which was the *preservation of memories.*

Similarly, *Encyclopaedia Britannica*, the gold standard among reference encyclopedias, could not survive the digital age. In order to compete with digital encyclopedias such as *Encarta* offered free by Microsoft as part of standard software on PCs, the company initially tried to sell high-priced CD-ROMs that were not well received by customers. They then moved to a subscriber-based web platform that could not compete with rapidly growing and cost-free *Wikipedia* that started in 2001 and gathered rapid momentum through the 2000s. In 2012, after 244 years, *Encyclopaedia Britannica* finally announced that they would no longer be in the print business. Their online website is struggling to compete with *Wikipedia* and the vast quantities of free content on the Internet.[89] Britannica overlooked the fact that their prestigious leather-bound gilt-edged 32-volume set had been substituted in the late 1990s at the same price point by sophisticated digital media such as PCs and increasingly at lower price points by laptops and tablets such as iPads that could provide authentic information in a more convenient and easier-to-access format to their consumers. Rather than focus on their *core capabilities of information gathering and authentication,* Britannica continued to invest in capabilities of printing, sales, and distribution of print-based books that did not add to the utility of customers looking for *accurate and credible reference information.*

Conversely, there are several cases of firms that were able to evolve and change to more sustainable business models and technologies to deliver their core consumer utility and value. During the 1990s, the concept of "negawatts" emerged among electric utilities. A "negawatt" (a term coined by Amory Lovins of the Rocky Mountain Institute) is a theoretical unit of power that represents the amount of energy (measured in watts) saved[90] mainly due to energy conservation and increased efficiency. Accelerating demand for energy, saturated power generation capacity, clean air regulations that capped carbon dioxide and sulfur dioxide emissions, and other environmental concerns placed severe limitations on building new power generation capacity to meet the rising demand in the northeast of the US during the early 1990s. The difficulties of adding supply to meet rising demand led to a realization that there was potential to manage demand for energy. New England Electric and other utilities began to work on conservation and energy efficiency programs for their industrial and residential customers. Thus, every 1,000 watt unit of power saved was a *negawatt* that led to a reduced demand and eliminated the need to add new capacity for *megawatts*. The energy efficiency and conservation led to shared cost savings for customers via reduced power bills and for the power utilities that could now use their funds to generate quicker and better returns than investing in capital-intensive power projects that had very long payback periods. In New England, demand-side conservation now competes on equal terms with power generation projects to fill the region's need for electricity. In 2008, a forward capacity auction held by the Independent System Operator-New England (ISO-NE) for the six-state region in the northeast US approved efficiency-related measures creating 1,188 MW of energy savings (negawatts) versus only 626 MW of proposed new power generation.[91] The efficiencies will cut growth in energy demand in the region by half over 15 years.[92]

A famous and often cited example of a company that developed a sustainable business model by focusing on its core business proposition is that of Interface Inc. The company used to sell broadloom carpet for business and industrial use. This carpet was traditionally replaced by customers every decade or so when it was completely worn out. This required a capital layout and led to a disruption of operations in customers' businesses when carpets were changed. Firms had to allocate capital expenditure to new carpets and incur costs in the disposal of old carpets in landfills. Moreover, the environmental impacts of the traditional carpet business are significant. The raw material is petroleum-based fiber. It takes over half a kilogram of fossil fuel to turn a quarter of a kilogram of fiber into a carpet. Fossil fuels are then used to transport the carpet to the customer, and eventually to a landfill where it decomposes over thousands of years.

Under the visionary leadership of the late Ray Anderson, its CEO, Interface changed its business model from selling carpets to *leasing floor comfort*. They realized that their business was to provide customers with aesthetic and comfortable floor surfaces rather than carpets. Under the changed business model, Interface's customers do not have to set aside capital outlays for buying new carpets every decade or so but can write off their lease expenses every month against their income. Interface now lays carpet tiles for customers and maintains ownership of the tiles and is responsible for keeping them fresh and clean. Interface's employees perform a monthly inspection and replace any carpet tiles that appear worn or stained. The tiles are self-stick, significantly reducing glue fumes used to lay traditional carpets. The model also converts the carpet business from a seasonal business when orders were placed at the end of the budget year to a steady year-round revenue stream. This business model is a win–win for all: the customers can write off lease charges against income and have consistently fresh-looking carpets, Interface's profits are higher due to the leasing fees and lower use of energy and raw materials, and the environment is cleaner due to significantly lower landfill disposal and lower material energy use.[93]

In order to further reduce its carbon footprint and to deal with competition from imitators, Interface developed a new floor covering called Solenium. Imitators of the Interface business model usually recycle their nylon and PVC-based carpets into a lower quality product. They thus lose the energy value of the nylon. However, Interface has developed a whole new polymeric material into a new kind of floor covering that can be completely recycled and remanufactured into itself. During the remanufacturing process, worn Solenium floor coverings are separated into their original components (fiber and backing) and remade into a fresh product. Virgin raw materials are not used in the process and remanufacturing the upper surface fibers with old material results in 99.7% less waste (the additional 0.3% is reused in other ways). This 100% recyclable product provides better customer utility, is highly stain resistant, and does not mildew. In addition, it is easily cleaned with water—unlike other carpets that require toxic cleaning solvents. The carpet is 35 percent less material-intensive, and yet lasts four times longer than other carpets. In ecological terms, compared with standard nylon broadloom carpet, Solenium has better physical attributes, reduced material use, and lower energy use by 97 percent, thus reducing costs and improving profits.[94]

The Interface process of developing a sustainable business model by focusing on its core business proposition is an excellent example of how firms can change if they focus on the customer solution that they provide rather than the product that they sell in order to develop sustainable business models. The changed business model delivers better customer utility, generates higher profits, builds competitive advantage, and significantly reduces the environmental footprint.

The Canadian steel company Dofasco struggled during the 1990s as a high-cost Canadian producer of steel competing against steel from China and South Korea. By adopting the sustainability lens of clean technology, the company was able to develop a sustainable logic among its managers that the customer utility that they provided was *not steel but rather structural strength* for their customers' products. Thus, its managers were able to innovate high value-added ultra-light (but structurally stronger) steels based on composite materials that differentiated Dofasco's products among its customers.[95] Dofasco's customers, mainly automobile companies in the Sothern Ontario-Michigan belt, preferred the ultra-light composite steels because they were lighter and stronger, enabling closer tolerances, lowering weight, and improving functional performance of finished car parts. Even though the cost per ton was higher than for conventional steel, the automobile companies needed to purchase a smaller quantity because of its lighter weight and hence were able to reduce their total cost of materials and reduce the weight of the automobile. Dofasco increased its profit margins significantly. Hence, in 2006, it became the subject of a takeover battle between ThyssenKrup of Germany and Arcelor Mittal of Luxembourg, with the latter company winning the battle. The innovation process has continued after the takeover with the development of an ultra-low carbon steel in 2010.[96]

Developing clarity of managerial thinking about how sustainability connects to the firm's core business proposition based on the consumer need that it addresses, and the utility/solutions that the firm's products and services provide, requires careful analysis and discussion. Answering the following questions effectively can help the process of arriving at a forward-looking understanding of these connections.

1. *What specific need does your product/service help the customer meet?* Does your customer need the electricity generated by coal or oil or does the customer need the energy required for running motors, devices, appliances, and to ensure a comfortable climate at home and at work? A little thought clarifies that it is the latter rather than the former but it is surprising that most managers working in utilities are obsessed about improving the efficiency and technology of the current operations and do not pay attention to the customer utility. Moreover, does the customer prefer to buy electricity from a large centralized utility located hundreds of miles away or rather prefer self-sufficiency based on renewable (e.g., solar) power and the ability to sell surplus power back to the grid? Again, it is likely to be the latter rather than the former. Yet, power companies continue to invest in, and develop, large centralized fossil fuel based power generation technologies that may become legacy sunk assets creating exit barriers.

2. *What specific problem does your product or service help your customer solve?* It may be tempting to assume that the answer to this question would be similar to the answer to the first question above. However, by focusing on the problem that the firm solves for the customer, multiple dimensions of a business model that can generate layers of competitive advantage become clear. In the case of Interface, for customers it solved the problem of not having to set aside funds for periodic capital expenditure to replace carpets. Its customers could now write off leasing charges every month against current income. It solved the problem and costs of disposal of used carpet. It solved the problem of stained and worn-out carpets by inspecting and replacing tiles every month. Finally, it provided the customer utility of an environmentally friendly product. Hence, it created layers of advantage and linked its customers integrally into its business model. A company that looks at its product purely as a carpet may focus on the weave, the colors, the patterns, the fiber, and other features that do not address the problems of the customer.

3. *Are there products or services in your industry or in another industry that can help your customers meet the same need or solve the same problem to the same or better extent or in cheaper ways?* Or are there emerging technologies that could provide your customers with better and/or cheaper solutions for their needs or problems? Are your competitors developing and adopting technologies that will enable them to deliver the same utility to your customers better and cheaper than you can? It is important to separate customer utility from the product—firms often focus on products being developed for customers rather than substitutes that can disrupt their products. Firms often lock themselves down into one technology and focus on selling the product(s) based on a continuous refinement of that technology.[97] They lose competitive

advantage or are disrupted as they are blindsided by new technologies that deliver the same utility to their customers better or more cheaply. On the other hand, a firm that is constantly focused on the customer utility it is delivering will be able to more easily identify new technologies that can deliver better or cheaper utility via sustainable products or business models to its own customers. As its customers copied its carpet-tile leasing model, Interface innovated a new type of floor covering, Solenium, that delivered superior value to customers and had a much lower environmental footprint. Increasingly, firms are using nanotechnologies and digital technologies to develop sustainable business models with significantly higher positive social and environmental impacts as compared to traditional centralized capital-intensive operations. For example, distributed solar and wind generation have a significantly lower environmental footprint and greater customer convenience and value as compared to huge centralized power plants with extensive distribution grids and significant transmission losses and inefficiencies.

4. *Are there business models or delivery mechanisms that could provide your customers with better or cheaper solutions for their needs or problems? Can you develop business models that integrate the consumer into a closed-loop value chain?* Interface tied the customer to the firm for the long term by providing the service of maintaining fresh and aesthetic floor comfort and taking back worn-out carpet tiles in a closed-loop operation. Similarly, cloud computing services tie a mobile device to certain providers such as Android or iTunes, etc. If a shoe company decides to go into the business of shoeing people for life, it integrates them into its closed-loop from the time they are children until their old age as it takes back old shoes, recycles the materials, and continuously provides them with shoes that meet their needs as they age and

as seasons change. This is steady continuous income and the company does not have to spend as many marketing dollars on acquiring new customers.

5. *Can you change your business model to substitute services for materials?* While Interface substituted leasing for traditional carpet as a conscious decision to reduce environmental impact, in other industries this may have happened as a normal process of technological development. For example, the travel and financial services businesses have substantially moved online. Cloud computing reduces the need for big personal computers with storage capacity and less material-intensive mobile devices can be used. It is surprising that shoe companies have not yet examined models to deliver services to "shoe" people for their entire lives instead of selling shoes. Car sharing can be taken to the next level by making different types and capacities of personal transportation run on hydrogen devices available for different needs of consumers at different times.

6. *Do alternate or substitute products, services, or technologies have the potential to have greater positive environmental and social impacts while generating competitive advantage?* It is critical that in innovating sustainable products and business models, managers do not lose sight of the potential of creating layers of advantage via generation of positive impacts on three dimensions: social, environmental, and financial, and not just on one dimensions. The business has to generate long-term shareholder value while generating social and environmental value.

Table 4.1 provides examples of how managers, in moving from a focus on customer need to customer utility delivered, can open their thinking to products and services that are not only more sustainable but also more competitive for the future.

Table 4.1 **Examples: Developing the core sustainable business proposition**

Customer need	Products/services	Capabilities	Customer utility	Products/services	Capabilities
Photographs	Cameras; film; photographic paper	Manufacturing; photo processing value chain	Preserving memories	Digital cameras; digital/cloud storage	Digital storage devices; alliances; plain paper printing
Floor covering	Carpets	Purchasing; manufacturing; sales; financing	Floor comfort & aesthetics	Recycled carpet tiles	Recycling; leasing; consumer servicing
Power	Electricity	Generation; distribution; retailing	Affordable/reliable energy; climate control	Distributed solar/wind	Manufacture/design; direct marketing; grid interface; alliances
Steel	Steel sheets, bars	Mining; purchasing; economies of scale	Structural strength	Composite materials; nanomaterials	R&D; flexible/batch manufacturing
Automobile	Cars	Design; economies of scale; automation; dealer network; financing	Mobility	Mass transit; car sharing	Alliances; distribution; consumer linking

An analysis of the core business proposition can point to several different pathways for the firm. Should it invest in a single future or should it adopt a portfolio of sustainable futures? The next section addresses this question.

Equating corporate value with sustainable value

In order to translate an understanding of the core business proposition into sustainable innovations, managers need a clear understanding of how the sustainable value that is created by the innovations adds to corporate value. Corporate value includes return on equity/sales/investment and other forms of value such as process efficiency, operational yields, risk and liability reduction in global supply chains, product innovation, market share, morale, and corporate reputation. As will be clear from Chapter 3, a sustainable strategy has the potential to lead to corporate value via eco-efficiency which results in waste and energy reduction and hence higher yields, risk and liability reduction along the value chain, eco-innovation, new markets and businesses, increased employee morale, and enhanced corporate reputation. Hence, sustainable innovation has the potential to simultaneously create value socially, environmentally, and financially.

In "Creating Sustainable Value," Hart and Milstein[98] presented a framework that argued that, in creating sustainable value, firms also generate traditional corporate value. The authors offered an analytical framework of a portfolio of four sustainable value strategies based on whether a firm focused its sustainability lens internally or externally and whether it focused the lens on its current businesses or future businesses.

According to these authors, in focusing the sustainability lens internally on their current business model, firms will follow a sustainability strategy of pollution control and pollution prevention (P2). They will generate corporate value in terms of reduced business risks and liabilities of environmental accidents and social conflicts, and reduced costs associated with lower wastes, material, and energy use (see Chapter 3 for a more detailed discussion of this strategy). Therefore, even at a basic level, a proactive sustainability strategy (versus a reactive compliance strategy) generates corporate value through lower risk, process efficiencies, higher production yields, and lower material and energy usage. Such a strategy is often referred to as an eco-efficiency strategy. As discussed in Chapter 3, it has been adopted by an increasing number of firms starting as far back as the 1970s with 3M's 3P program (Pollution Prevention Pays). Such a strategy is based on continuous but incremental improvement within the firm's current business model and does not position the firm for competitive advantage in the future. This strategy is also easily imitable and hence, after a firm reaps the low hanging fruit of cost savings, further benefits require increasingly larger investments for generating ever-smaller gains. Nevertheless, a large proportion of the firms in almost all industries currently adopt this strategy, especially those with large quantities of wastes and emissions such as chemical companies (and hence, the early adoption by 3M, Dow, and DuPont). This is an easy strategy to adopt since it does not involve changes to the current business model.

Firms that focus the sustainability lens on their current business model but are outward looking and engage their external stakeholders such as customers and suppliers in the process of developing and implementing their sustainability strategy will be likely to develop a sustainability strategy of managing the sustainability impacts of their product or service life-cycles. This strategy of product stewardship is designed to address the concerns of a firm's customers and other stakeholders about the sustainability impacts during the transportation, consumption, and disposal of its products and also the extraction, growing, manufacture, and transportation of their inputs. Firms seek to engage their suppliers and customers to develop mutually satisfactory sustainability practices such as supply chain sustainability analysis and product life-cycle analysis. This strategy involves incremental innovations via eco-design. This strategy generates cost savings via reduction of packaging, materials, and energy usage but also creates corporate value by helping the firm enhance the reputation and legitimacy of its operations. As described in Chapter 3, companies such as Procter & Gamble have been pioneers in this type of sustainability strategy. This strategy usually does not involve changes in the current business model.

Firms may choose to diversify into new businesses based on clean and environmentally friendly new technologies. For example, oil companies such as BP and Shell have invested substantially to develop new businesses based on solar, wind, geothermal, biofuels, and tidal wave energy; automobile companies such as Toyota, Ford, Honda, Nissan, and GM have diversified into electric and hybrid engines and are developing hydrogen fuel-cell based engines; paper companies are exploring liquid LED-based flexible displays; and steel companies such as Canada's Dofasco have diversified into ultra-light steels and carbon composite materials that are stronger but much less material-intensive. This is a diversification strategy where the firm adds environmentally friendly products and technologies to its portfolio and positions itself to compete in the future. This process may involve the adoption of existing technologies or the development and adoption of radical new technologies that could generate revenues, profits, and competitive advantage in the future.

Firms may choose to focus not only on new clean technologies and products but may also follow a strategy to develop sustainable business models for emerging markets with unmet needs, that is, at the base of the income pyramid where people earn between one and three dollars a day. These firms are better prepared to address the complete definition of sustainable development according to the Brundtland Commission, which requires firms to simultaneously make positive impacts on social justice by reducing poverty and the natural environment by providing clean water, clean air, energy security, health, communication, and education. These companies are the ones that will eventually come closest to the definition of a sustainable organization. The development of sustainable business models targeted toward markets with extremely low disposable income, poor distribution infrastructure, and low profit margins have the potential to generate new technologies, products, and business models that have the potential to be scaled up to developed markets and disrupt traditional industries.[99] While several firms are developing business models in this space, only a few have succeeded in generating positive economic, social, and environmental impacts. A prime example is the Grameen Bank in Bangladesh. Others such as GE have developed products such as the Vscan that delivers healthcare scans at low cost to the poor in villages and has been scaled up to meet the needs of developed markets as well. A large number of small entrepreneurs and start-ups have begun to scale up their sustainable business models in the base of the pyramid. This will be discussed in Chapter 7.

Generating a sustainable portfolio

Having developed an understanding of its core business proposition based on the utility delivered to its customers, the firm has to determine how to continue to deliver utility to its customers more effectively, competitively, and sustainably than its competitors.

The Hart and Milstein[100] framework presents a portfolio of approaches to create sustainable value for the firm and its stakeholders while competing successfully in delivering its core business proposition. The four quadrants of the sustainable value portfolio are not mutually exclusive and the firm does not have to choose only one over the others. Most firms cannot abruptly shut down their current operations. They have to begin by reducing and eliminating negative salient social and environmental impacts that are the most relevant to its current business (Chapter 2). This is the pollution prevention approach. At the same time, the concerns of the firm's salient stakeholders about the impacts of the firm's operations and its value chain (suppliers, distributors, and customers) have to be addressed via product stewardship approaches. While the firm actively develops strategies and practices to reduce or eliminate its negative social and environmental impacts via pollution prevention and product stewardship, it has at the same time to position itself for generating sustainable value in the future by developing and adopting new business models and clean technologies. This requires investments in research and development, alliances, and pilot projects to tap the vast opportunities in base of the pyramid markets. Engagement in the base of pyramid markets has the potential to generate further new technologies and business models in an escalating path of increasing sustainable value. This will be discussed in Chapter 7.

Summary

Developing sustainable business logic is the process of developing a shared organizational understanding of how the creation of social and environmental value also creates economic and shareholder value. Managers need to begin this process by developing a clear under-standing of the customer utility delivered and the customer problem solved rather than focusing on the product manufactured or service delivered. This helps identify emerging technologies, products, substi-tutes, and business models that can satisfy the same customer need or utility better and more sustainably. At the same time, a shared under-standing of customer utility helps managers understand the existing capabilities that can be leveraged for addressing sustainability chal-lenges and the ones that need to be acquired or developed. Sustainable business logic creates an organizational environment within which it is possible to change traditional thinking and mind-sets of managers and employees and begin a process of organizational change. The next chapter (Chapter 5) addresses how managerial mind-sets can be changed and opportunity frames created by organizations to spark sustainable innovation. Chapter 6 discusses the development of new, and leveraging of existing, capabilities to innovate sustainable strate-gies, products, and business models.

Five

Building motivation: Opportunity framing of sustainability challenges

Some see it as a threat, some see it as an opportunity and some see it as inevitable.

Stanley Fischer, *International Monetary Fund Deputy Managing Director, June 2000*

The most creative ideas for sustainable products, services, processes, and business models have the potential to come from a firm's managers who intimately understand the firm's business, customers, processes, and capabilities. Instead, most firms compartmentalize and assign the creative process to a small group of people, often in the research and development function. The bulk of a firm's creative talent (that is, its operational managers) is usually tied up with the day-to-day operations and routines of the current business. It rarely has the "white space" to apply fresh ideas and strategic thinking in innovating to compete effectively for a sustainable future. Even when managers understand the fundamental business logic that can help them change their frames of reference about their business, markets, and customers, they often stay locked into conventional patterns of thinking and decision-making. They default toward seeing changes in the business environment as a threat to their daily routines. Rather, innovation is based on the ability to see change as an opportunity, not a threat. This chapter explains why managers find it difficult to change their strategic thinking and how firms can overcome these biases by creating an opportunity frame within which innovative thinking can take place.

Being engaged in repetitious daily routines, managers often tend to default toward applying standard solutions and using rules of thumb to tackle emerging issues and problems. Their tendency is to resort to decision-making based on automatic responses that require little concentration and effort. Thus, during day-to-day operations, managers make decisions based on certain heuristics and rules of thumb without giving much thought to the uniqueness of the specific problem or issue. Such automatic or mindless decisions do not lead to choices that managers need to evaluate in order to analyze different courses of action and their implications for a firm's performance. According to research on individual decision-making by Kahneman and Tversky, innovative thinking requires decisions that are effortful, based on cognitive stress, concentration, and engaging of the mind. Such decisions lead to choices and evaluation of alternatives to determine the most effective actions rather than automatic responses.[101]

The lack of cognitive stress among managers is due to the fact that they have daily routines that occupy most of their time. They therefore tend to rely mainly on available and easily accessible information. Managers do not usually undertake the effort to conduct research to develop a full set of alternatives based on complete information. Thus, managers who are often pressed for time not only adopt rules of thumb but also extrapolate from personal experience and anecdotes, and overweight dramatic and salient events while underweighting rare events.

Kahneman and Tversky[102] conducted several experiments to show how managers routinely make decisions without cognitive stress. In one study they asked the question "*How many animals of each kind*

did Moses take into the Ark?" Without exception, in many different national contexts, the answer to the question from different sets
of participants from different organizations (including students in
universities, members of the armed forces, and managers in various
organizations) was "two." In their experiments, they did not come
across individuals who were able to exercise cognitive stress to make
an effort to realize that it was Noah who built the Ark and not Moses.
Another example described in Kahneman's book *Thinking Fast and
Slow* is a simple problem *"A bat and ball cost $1.10. The bat costs one
dollar more than the ball. How much does the ball cost?"* Once again,
this is a very simple problem well within the grasp of the abilities of
almost all managers in organizations. However, in experiments, most
got the incorrect answer of 10 cents. If the ball cost 10 cents and the
bat cost a dollar more, it would cost $1.10 and hence the total would
be $1.20. The correct answer is 5 cents.[103]

While the two examples provided above may seem simplistic, they
illustrate starkly how much more important it becomes to exercise cognitive stress in day-to-day decision-making when complex problems are
involved. When managers have to make decisions to simultaneously
deliver social, environmental, and economic value, significant cognitive
stress is required. Of course, the onus for generating cognitive stress
should not rest solely on managers but also on the firms that have to
create the white space,[104] opportunities, and incentives for more effortful and thoughtful decision-making in everyday workflow to generate alternate choices. In order for firms to make appropriate changes
in their organizations to foster creative thinking and innovation, they
must first understand why managers make biased decisions. The most
common sources of managerial decision bias are discussed below.

Halo effects

In the absence of research and the development and consideration
of different alternatives, it is common for managers to be influenced
by first impressions. There is an old proverb, "never judge a book

by its cover," and yet managers responsible for strategic resource allocations often succumb to first impressions. Such influence significantly limits debate and discussion. Decisions are often made on an initial personal like or dislike of an individual or an opportunity or a project. In psychology this is called the halo effect or "halo error" as described by Edward Thorndike.[105] In numerous experiments performed by psychologists, this effect has been shown in multiple contexts and situations. In a study by Kahneman and Tversky, when two different characters with identical personality traits are described to participants, with the list of traits reversed for one character, the participants express a preference for the individual with positive traits listed ahead of negative traits. The first character was described as "intelligent, industrious, impulsive, critical, stubborn and envious" while the second was "envious, stubborn, critical, impulsive, industrious, intelligent;" The experiment was performed with different groups and a statistically significant majority of participants preferred the first individual, clearly influenced by the first one or two traits.

This illustrates not only a halo effect but also the lack of cognitive stress and effort on the part of participants. If managers have to exercise cognitive stress to develop deep understanding of how to apply sustainable logic to products, services, processes, and business models that deliver value to customers, investors, society, and the environment, firms need to provide the space and opportunity for managers not only to develop but to evaluate complete information so that they do not make decisions based on first impressions or the most salient data.

Anchoring effects

Anchoring occurs when individuals use an initial piece of information to make subsequent judgments. The initial information becomes the anchor around which other judgments are made by adjusting away from that anchor. There is then a bias in interpreting other information around the anchor. For example, the initial asking price for a used automobile sets the standard for the rest of the negotiations, so that prices lower than the initial price seem more reasonable even if they are still higher than what the auto is really worth. This decision bias, identified by Kahneman and Tversky,[106] found that individuals rely overly on a specific piece of information or a reference point to govern their thought process. Once the anchor or reference point is set, there is a bias toward adjusting or interpreting other information to reflect the anchored information. The anchor can affect future decision-making and information analysis.

In an experiment that I conducted with two separate groups of forty managers in an executive MBA program, I asked each group the same question while changing the reference point. I asked the first group *"Are expected costs of carbon taxes to your business over the next 10 years more or less than $100,000?"* and I asked the other group *"Are expected costs of carbon taxes to your business over the next 10 years more or less than $100,000,000?"* Not surprisingly, the average estimates from the first group of managers from diverse industries was around the $100,000 reference point, ranging from $50,000 to $200,000, and the average estimates from the second group ranged between $75,00,000 to $150,000,000. Even though 10 to 20 percent of the EMBA students in each group were marketing professionals, they could not overcome this bias. This is surprising because anchoring is a trick that marketers use to signal the worth of a product to consumers. While marketing professionals in firms understand how anchoring affects consumer decisions, they themselves fall prey to anchoring biases in strategic decisions.

Loss bias

Kahneman and Tversky are most well-known for their work on loss bias, which they termed prospect theory. Daniel Kahneman won the 2002 Nobel Prize for Economic Sciences primarily for this work. Since Nobel prizes are not awarded posthumously, Tversky, who died in 1996, did not receive the award for their co-authored work.

Prospect theory describes how individuals choose between alternatives that involve risk, that is, where the probabilities of outcomes are known. Kahneman and Tversky argued that people make decisions based on the potential value of losses and gains rather than the final outcome. Their research confirmed in different contexts that, in general, possible losses loom twice as large as possible gains and managers usually tend to stick with the status quo to avoid potential loss. For example, people tended to overweight the 10 percent probability of mortality a month after a surgery and underweight the identical 90 percent probability of survival a month after that surgery.

My research in the North American oil and gas industry during the 1990s found that when managers in an oil and gas firm interpreted environmental issues as a threat, their firm was likely to adopt a reactive environmental strategy that focused on minimum legal compliance and pollution control; and when managers interpreted environmental issues as opportunities, their firm was likely to adopt a proactive environmental strategy[107] that included pollution prevention and clean technologies. This research showed that when managers viewed environmental issues as threats, they also viewed them as negative, as a source of potential loss to their performance on the job and to their organizational performance, and as uncontrollable.[108] On the other hand, when they viewed environmental issues as opportunities, they viewed them as positive, as a source of potential gain for their performance on the job and for their organizational performance, and as controllable.[109]

The study found a link between:

- Managers adopting a gain versus loss bias

- Positive versus negative bias

- Controllable versus uncontrollable bias

and the managers' interpretation of environmental issues and situations as opportunities versus threats. More importantly, their interpretation of environmental issues as an opportunity versus as a threat influenced whether their firm was proactive in its strategy (and thus innovated its products, services, and business models) to manage changing environments or whether it was reactive, defensive, and resisted change.

Overweighting of losses also leads to the strengthening of sunk cost bias by managers. Sunk costs are costs that have already been incurred and cannot be recovered. In traditional microeconomic theory, only prospective (future) costs are relevant to an investment decision. A rational manager should not allow sunk costs to influence her decisions. However, research has shown that such costs do influence managerial decision-making due to loss aversion.[110] For example, many individuals tend to hold on to equity stocks long after their values have fallen to irrecoverable levels, in the hope that prices will rise again.

Thus, as managers face the prospect of having to make more complex decisions that require consideration of not only economic but also social and environmental metrics, it is likely that they will view these decisions as negative, a source of loss, and uncontrollable. The next section explains how organizations can foster opportunity framing of such decisions by managers to spark innovations in sustainable processes, products, and business models.

Opportunity framing of sustainability challenges

Addressing sustainability challenges for firms and managers requires balancing short-term financial, social, and environmental performance while innovating to achieve future long-term financial, social, and environmental performance. This is much more complex than the focus that firms have traditionally had on optimum utilization of current assets to maximize financial performance in the short term. The need to balance short-term and long-term economic, social, and environmental performance leads to managers facing many more decision

variables and factors that they have to consider in a business environment that is volatile, uncertain, complex, and ambiguous (VUCA).
In such an environment, the decision rules of thumb that have been
used by managers earlier are ineffective. Effective decisions in such
a context require the generation of cognitive stress, search for information, experimentation, and innovation. This requires managerial
sense-making, that is, managers need to interpret and analyze how
the several factors and variables in the environment will individually
affect their business, and also how interactions among the factors will
affect the firm.

Innovations that will enable the firm to balance short-term and
long-term economic, social, and environmental performance require
organizational learning. This process involves harnessing information
from a variety of external stakeholders, combining the external information with internal information and knowledge within the firm,
generating new frames of decision-making reference, learning about
potential solutions, and fostering a process of experimentation and
continuous innovation. While Chapter 6 will focus on the capabilities
that firms need in order to generate proactive sustainability strategies
and innovations, the focus in this section is on how organizations can
ensure that managerial mind-sets are attuned toward opportunities
for developing innovative solutions rather than toward resisting the
threat of change and adopting defensive and reactive strategies.

Since busy managers tend to interpret major changes in their environment as threats to their perfected routines, and since threats generally loom twice as large as opportunities, organizations that seek
to generate innovative solutions to sustainability challenges need to
transform threat perceptions to opportunity perceptions. This is what
I refer to as the creation of an "opportunity frame" within the organization.[111] Opportunity frames require changing managerial perceptions of sustainability challenges as a source of loss, as negative, and
as uncontrollable to perceptions of solutions to these challenges as
sources of gain, as positive, and as controllable. My research in the
North American oil and gas industry[112] found that firms fostered

an opportunity frame for decision-making by making the following changes in their organizations.

Legitimization of sustainability in corporate identity

Managers' perceptions of their company's identity have been shown to influence how they interpret strategic issues, and thus indirectly influence organizational actions and strategies. When concern for the environment becomes an integral component of corporate identity, environmental issues become harder to disown.[113] A change in the corporate identity that explicitly includes a concern for sustainability (social and environmental impacts) makes it more possible and more likely that the firm sends the appropriate signals to managers. It becomes easier and legitimate to channel resources to the development of sustainability practices and innovations and justifies further commitment and allocation of resources. When managers perceive their organization's identity as partially or wholly focused on addressing sustainability challenges, finding solutions to deliver triple bottom-line performance will assume importance and lead to positive emotional linkages to sustainability practices. Companies can affect this change by changing their mission or vision statement and signaling to its managers that action on sustainability is important for the organization.

Some companies begin with social and/or environmental or sustainability enshrined in their mission statement. For example, Patagonia's mission has always emphasized environmental preservation (*"Build the best product, cause no unnecessary harm, use business to inspire and implement solutions to the environmental crisis"*)[114] and the Body Shop was set up to *"operate our business with a strong commitment to the well being of our fellow humans and the preservation of the planet."*[115] Changing an existing corporate mission to drive managerial decisions requires extensive and repeated communication, widely across the organization. Recently Unilever, under its CEO Paul Polman, established a mission to double profits while halving environmental impact. Polman has used every opportunity to publicize this as a part of Unilever's identity.[116]

DuPont changed its mission from a company focused on chemical production to a mission, vision, and values with sustainability in the core of each.[117]

> *Dupont's Mission*: Sustainable Growth: The creation of shareholder and societal value while we reduce our environmental footprint along the value chains in which we operate.
>
> *DuPont's Vision*: Our vision is to be the world's most dynamic science company, creating sustainable solutions essential to a better, safer, healthier life for people everywhere.
>
> *DuPont's Values*: Safety, concern and care for people, protection of the environment and personal and corporate integrity, are this company's highest values, and we will not compromise them.

The change in mission was a critical signal to all managers of DuPont to begin to perform on the triple bottom line as an important part of their job. Paul Tebo, the former Corporate Vice-President of Safety, Health and Environment at DuPont, was told by the CEO Chad Holliday to work toward a target where his position would not be required, and all of DuPont's managers would take on the responsibility for the environmental, health, and safety mission of the firm.[118] Regardless, the change in mission did not happen overnight and took several months of communication and discussion among members of the top management team.

Ben & Jerry's mission statement comprehensively brings together the economic, social, and environmental elements of sustainability. Even though Ben & Jerry's is now owned by Unilever, it operates as an autonomous company with an independent mission. The firm converted in 2012 to a B-corp (benefit corporation registered in the US as a nonprofit that uses the power of business to solve social and environmental problems) so that it can focus on delivering value to multiple stakeholders instead of only to shareholders. The company now reports its performance on governance and impacts on workers, community, and the environment.[119] The Ben & Jerry's website[120] contains the following mission statement:

> Ben & Jerry's is founded on and dedicated to a sustainable corporate concept of linked prosperity. Our mission consists of 3 interrelated parts:
>
> *Social Mission*: To operate the Company in a way that actively recognizes the central role that business plays in society by initiating innovative ways to improve the quality of life locally, nationally and internationally.
>
> *Product Mission*: To make, distribute and sell the finest quality all natural ice cream and euphoric concoctions with a continued commitment to incorporating wholesome, natural ingredients and promoting business practices that respect the Earth and the Environment.
>
> *Economic Mission*: To operate the Company on a sustainable financial basis of profitable growth, increasing value for our stakeholders and expanding opportunities for development and career growth for our employees.
>
> Underlying the mission of Ben & Jerry's is the determination to seek new and creative ways of addressing all three parts, while holding a deep respect for individuals inside and outside the company and for the communities of which they are a part. We have a progressive, nonpartisan social mission that seeks to meet human needs and eliminate injustices in our local, national and international communities by integrating these concerns into our day-to-day business activities. Our focus is on children and families, the environment and sustainable agriculture on family farms.
>
> *Values*:
>
> Capitalism and the wealth it produces do not create opportunity for everyone equally. We recognize that the gap between the rich and the poor is wider than at any time since the 1920's. We strive to create economic opportunities for those who have been denied them and to advance

new models of economic justice that are sustainable and replicable.

By definition, the manufacturing of products creates waste. We strive to minimize our negative impact on the environment.

The growing of food is overly reliant on the use of toxic chemicals and other methods that are unsustainable. We support sustainable and safe methods of food production that reduce environmental degradation, maintain the productivity of the land over time, and support the economic viability of family farms and rural communities.

We seek and support nonviolent ways to achieve peace and justice. We believe government resources are more productively used in meeting human needs than in building and maintaining weapons systems.

We strive to show a deep respect for human beings inside and outside our company and for the communities in which they live.

With such a comprehensive statement of corporate identity, it is not surprising that every employee of Ben & Jerry's is motivated to work toward sustainable practices and innovations.

Some companies reinforce sustainable thinking by finding avenues for their managers to experience environmental loss and social injustice first hand. The Tata Group of companies in India for decades has required its managers to spend time in rural areas to experience how 70 percent of India's billion-plus people live. This has led to changed mind-sets toward finding sustainable solutions to business problems and has generated several sustainable product and business models. For example, the Tata-BP Solar joint venture's managers have learnt from such experiences to develop businesses to deliver energy to the rural poor including solar home lighting systems, solar lanterns, solar cookers, and solar hot water systems.[121] Tata Solar's other products include: Sunbank, a customized package that runs computers in rural banks and consists of a power pack along with solar modules, batteries and controllers, and provides power for three to six hours a day; a power pack to run rural ATMs; Suraksha, a solar-powered communication system to help police stations function effectively; Arogya, a solar-powered vaccine refrigerator for rural health centers manufactured indigenously by the company and approved by the World Health Organization (WHO); Tejas, a solar power generator to power computers, TVs, lights, and fans in rural schools; a low-cost solar lantern priced at $27; and a 40 to 50 liters rural solar water heater priced at $80. It is the first-hand experience in rural markets and a sustainability mission that enables Tata's managers to identify ideas for sustainable innovation. These innovations have been co-created with the poor in base of the pyramid markets in India. Such innovations are the focus of Chapter 7.

The greater the extent to which addressing sustainability challenges is central or core to the corporate identity, the greater the extent to which managers will view actions, decisions, and solutions to such challenges as positive[122] rather than negative, *changing this element of threat perception to an opportunity interpretation.*

Integration of social and environmental metrics into performance evaluation

Managers searching for, and experimenting with, sustainability solutions and new technologies face high outcome uncertainty. This means that managers are not sure how new innovations will impact the firm's economic performance and affect their own job performance. Innovative processes, products, business models, and technologies may yield positive economic performance and returns only over a long-term period and carry a threat of failure for managers. This increases the possibility of a negative impact on their performance and may jeopardize their job, enhancing threat perceptions. Firms need to address managerial interpretations of sustainability issues as potential losses by adding social and environmental criteria to their performance evaluation. For experimental projects or radical new technologies, even the economic performance criteria should require a lower rate of return initially, longer-term expectations or returns, and a holistic evaluation of employee performance rather than a short-term and narrow focus on monthly and quarterly economic (sales, output, profits) performance. Balancing the long-term, output-based economic, social, and environmental performance criteria with short-term economic criteria in employee performance evaluation encourages managers to address sustainability challenges as an opportunity for gain rather than as a threat of loss. Rewarding managers for achieving long-term sustainability targets reduces the possibility that managers will associate the unpredictability and risk of their actions in the short term as a threat of loss.

To illustrate, in 2010, Unilever established a goal to halve the environmental impact of each brand while doubling sales by 2020.[123] Similarly, in 2002, DuPont set four specific goals to evaluate employees on their sustainability performance, each with a target date of 2010. The first was to derive 25 percent of its revenues from non-depletable resources such as agricultural feedstocks, up from about 10 percent in 2002 and up from 5 percent in its base year, 1998. The second was to reduce its global carbon-equivalent greenhouse gas emissions by 65 percent using 1990 as a base year. The third was to hold total energy-use flat, using 1990 as a base year, thereby offsetting all production increases with corresponding improvements in energy efficiency. The fourth was to source 10 percent of its global energy use in the year 2010 from renewable resources.[124]

Chad Holliday, the former Chairman and CEO of DuPont, propagated SVA (shareholder value added) as a performance evaluation criterion. This was defined as the shareholder value created above the cost of capital (which typically is 10 to 12 percent for corporations in the United States) based mainly on the addition of knowledge. As per DuPont's targets, the higher the SVA per pound of production, the greater the knowledge intensity in creating economic value. Along with more traditional financial measures like return on invested capital and cash flow, this metric provided a useful indicator of the long-term sustainability of different growth strategies.[125]

Siemens' Performance Review Process and the Siemens Management Review, a standard practice company-wide, enables management-level and non-managerial employees alike to set clear personal goals on economic, social, and environmental performance and to give and receive continuous, open feedback. These provide a transparent measure of employees' sustainability performance and accomplishments and, as such, determine future career development and remuneration.[126]

As more managers within a firm interpret sustainability challenges as opportunities, these issues become increasingly legitimized as a component of their corporate identity and reinforce the organizational actions and practices that enable the successful management of these issues. This generates a virtuous cycle. If a firm's sustainability strategy is considered successful, and if it continues to balance economic, social, and ecological performance well, then managerial interpretations of sustainability issues as opportunities will be further reinforced. Conversely, continued losses may force a re-evaluation of corporate identity and the organizational design and may reinforce negative managerial interpretations of sustainability challenges as potentially being an uncontrollable threat of loss. My research in the North American oil and gas industry confirmed that the more a company integrated environmental performance criteria into its performance evaluation, the greater was the likelihood that its managers interpreted environmental issues as *opportunities rather than as threats*.[127]

Discretionary slack

To manage the threat associated with the unpredictability inherent in the search for, and adoption of, innovative sustainability solutions (technologies, products, services, business models) managers require a measure of discretionary resources and time. Discretion is the latitude of managerial action[128] and slack is the "resource that enables an organization both to adjust to gross shifts in the external environment with minimal trauma, and to experiment with new postures in relation to that environment, either through new product introductions or through innovations in management style."[129] Thus, discretionary slack is a combination of the time and resources that facilitate desired strategic or creative behavior within an organization and allow managers to adjust and respond to changes in the external environment.

Not all types of slack may help generate sustainable innovations. Only "high discretion slack" in the form of free time and resources can be applied to a wide variety of situations and problems and facilitates problem-solving behavior. In contrast, "low discretion slack," in the form of idle machines, excess production capacity, and idle personnel who are highly specialized in specific tasks, has very specific applications and may be difficult to adapt[130] for generating sustainable innovations. High discretion slack enables managers to increase their perceived sense of controllability to manage the threats associated with the unpredictability and risk of searching for, and adopting, innovative sustainability practices and technologies.

A company well known for fostering innovation by providing its managers with discretionary slack is 3M.[131] 3M's goal is to generate one-third of its sales every year through new products. Correspondingly, it provides its senior managers with almost one-third of their budgets and time as discretionary. This enables them to experiment with, and develop, new products and services. The firm adopts a long-term approach to the new product development process by creating a culture of innovation that encourages risk-taking, tolerates mistakes made along the way, and rewards achievement. A culture of innovation means that senior management encourages employees to spend a significant portion of their time on experimentation and research that goes beyond their usual scope of responsibilities. This involves hosting ideation sessions in which the innovation champion creates an environment of trust and openness. Only by breaking out of their usual comfort zones can teams create truly disruptive technology. As part of the company's holistic innovation strategy, 3M aims to develop disruptive innovations outside of the current existing portfolio. In 2008, 3M began strategically investing in startups with long-term benefit to the company, resulting in collaborations and increased technological development for sustainable innovations. These 3M New Ventures includes Energy Inc., which monitors residential and commercial energy consumption to reduce costs and energy use.[132]

3M capitalizes on its innovation success by combining diverse technologies in new and unexpected ways. It draws upon innovative technologies from its portfolio of 55,000 products to create new sustainable solutions, such as applying dental technology to innovations in less material-intensive components for automobiles. By making these uncommon connections, the company pioneers new ways of innovating. The use of discretionary slack is meant for long-term, sustained innovation with dedicated R&D, long-term development, ideation sessions with members of all departments, fostering a culture of innovation by allowing team members to take risks in a protected environment, and rewarding and encouraging creativity. Similarly, companies such as DuPont and Google provide their managers with discretionary slack resources and time to find solutions to achieve their sustainability targets.

The greater the degree of discretionary slack provided to managers in managing sustainability challenges, the greater the likelihood that they will interpret these challenges as opportunities rather than as threats because they now have control over resources and time to experiment and innovate. *The uncontrollability dimension in the threat perception changes to controllability in an opportunity perception.*

Information flow

As managers begin to balance short-term economic performance with long-term economic, social, and environmental metrics, there are considerable uncertainties and ambiguities regarding the evolving regulations, societal expectations, and appropriate technologies. There is a great deal of uncertainty about the relationship between organizational actions and performance outcomes. Even if managers know the right questions to ask, the information and knowledge necessary to answer these questions is not readily available. Without this information, the financial and technical implications of a decision are difficult to assess. When managers have to deliver on social and environmental metrics, they still have to deliver on financial and technical metrics. Hence managers experience a lack of control and a threat perception in managing sustainability challenges.

Firms deal with this uncertainty by developing detailed and specific measures of their sustainability footprint (see Chapter 2), developing detailed and specific performance targets, and undertaking detailed environmental audits using certified third parties to clearly show managers where the firm stands as compared to its peers (benchmarks) and targets. Firms make this information publicly available to all employees and sometimes to other stakeholders via sustainability reports. While the staff-level legal and sustainability departments may be responsible for initial generation of this information, subsequent knowledge generation and solutions involve line managers at all levels, sparking a fast pace of learning. Just as in the example of DuPont where the VP (EHS) Paul Tebo was asked to eliminate the staff-level function by making sustainability everyone's job, line managers need to become the primary sources of knowledge for finding solutions for sustainability challenges.

Because line managers tend to emphasize economic and operational targets while staff managers tend to emphasize the interpretation and analysis of sustainability regulations, new technologies and societal expectations, it is important to strike a balance of influence between line and staff units in formulating sustainability strategies. Companies with successful strategies achieve this via the use of such integrative devices as cross-functional committees, task forces, and rotation of staff officers to the business units. This balancing of responsibilities for information support sparks processes of learning and knowledge generation for sustainable innovation. This alleviates the feeling of lack of control, and, armed with sufficient information about the technologies and best practices that can help the firm address sustainability challenges, managers now *perceive these as opportunities*.

Selling sustainable logic

The desired outcome of creating an opportunity frame is to foster a bubbling of ideas for sustainable innovations in products, services, and business models from the grassroots of the firm. At the same time, the top management team may have its own priorities for sustainable businesses. How does an idea rise to the top and have a chance of attracting resources for implementation? Which ideas are more likely to succeed? My research in multiple contexts including banks, forestry companies, oil companies, and consumer products companies has shown that pushing an idea down from the top management without laying groundwork at middle management levels has a low chance of success. Business ideas are implemented at the middle manager level. Therefore, ideas that are pushed down from top management without a champion(s) at the middle management level may stagnate, even though these ideas may be supported by the resources necessary for implementation. Such ideas are likely to enter the formal resource allocation process too soon, before a strong feasibility has been established and without buy-in by a critical mass of middle managers who are absolutely essential for effective implementation. In fact, innovations pushed down from the top without a support base at lower levels of the organization may have the effect that is opposite of the desired one. Managers who have not bought in to these ideas may perceive them as a threat to their job and may not pour in their maximum effort to implement these ideas in innovative and effective ways.

On the other hand, sustainable innovations initiated by middle managers can have the greatest possibility of success if they are carefully and effectively sold to peers and superiors. The successful ideas start at the middle of an organization that has created an opportunity frame to foster experimentation and research for sustainable innovation. Before resources are allocated, the managers use informal channels to build peer support among other managers. They also use other managers as sounding boards for these ideas. Their peers also help them develop a strong feasibility and business case for the innovation. For example, during my research in the Royal Bank of Canada during the mid 2000s, I found that several innovative businesses with positive social impacts were successful because the initiators of these business ideas worked informally with risk management experts within the bank to develop the feasibility of the ideas. Risk management is a key decision variable and a key capability in banks and financial institutions. Working informally with a network of middle managers and external experts, middle managers built a strong feasibility for the innovation that fit the bank's core mission and values. It was only at this stage that the innovations entered the formal channels to seek resource allocations from the top management. At this stage, the innovation's feasibility had been developed from different perspectives, the middle managers had bought into the innovation and were ready to support implementation, and, in some cases, pilot projects had already been tested. Thus, these ideas had improved their probability of successful implementation significantly.

While the bias of this chapter is toward creating an opportunity frame within organizations to spark creative thinking and sustainable innovations, similar principles apply for entrepreneurs seeking to sell sustainable innovations to investors and other stakeholders. They need to understand the decision biases of investors and venture capitalists and develop proposals that transfer threat perceptions of new innovations into opportunities to be supported.

Summary

Even if a firm develops a clear business logic around the importance of addressing sustainability challenges, managers find it difficult to make decisions to innovate for sustainable products and business models due to several decision-making biases that they are subject to within their day-to-day organizational contexts. Due to severe time constraints, they rarely generate cognitive stress in day-to-day decision-making and undertake many decisions on auto-pilot, using rules of thumb and other heuristics such as halo effects, using salient facts and anecdotes rather than complete data, anchoring biases, and most importantly a significant overweighting of potential losses versus possible gains. Losses often loom twice as large as gains. Hence, managers often view sustainability challenges as threats to be averted rather than as opportunities to be seized. Threats versus opportunities have three dimensions: negative versus positive, loss versus gain, and uncontrollable versus controllable. In order to overcome these three dimensions of threat perceptions, firms need to create an opportunity frame by legitimizing sustainability in their corporate identity, evaluating employees on sustainability (economic, social, and environmental) performance metrics, creating discretionary slack to enable employees to experiment and innovate, and empowering employees with detailed information, specific measurement of the firm's sustainability footprint, and specific and time-bound targets. Firms also need to create mechanisms for idea generation and knowledge development on sustainable solutions by fostering active interaction between staff and line (operational) managers. Figure 5.1 shows this process graphically.

Figure 5.1 **Creating an opportunity frame**

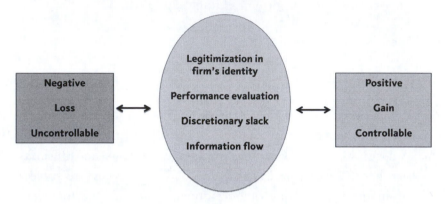

To improve the probability for success of sustainable innovations in firms that have created opportunity frames, ideas should be encouraged to emerge at the middle of the organization and managers given the time and discretion to get their peers to informally buy in to the ideas and help them develop a strong feasibility and business case. It is only at that stage that these ideas should enter the formal resource allocation process for implementation.

Having developed a business logic to adopt a sustainable strategy and having created an opportunity frame within which managers are motivated to view sustainability challenges as opportunities, the firm has the *motivation* to become a sustainable organization. However, it still needs the *capacity* to translate the motivation into practices and action. This capacity requires the development of organizational capabilities that are unique to the firm. These critical capabilities are discussed in the next chapter.

Six

Building capacity: Critical capabilities for sustainable innovation

Let your plans be dark and impenetrable as night...

Sun Tzu, *Art of War*

It is widely accepted in scholarly and popular business literature that a firm's internal resources and capabilities can generate significant competitive advantage for firms. Capabilities are unique ways in which a firm combines and deploys some of its tangible and intangible assets, processes, and systems to achieve superior outcomes and innovations than its competitors. The real value of capabilities lies in their being impenetrable to competitors and hard to imitate because they reside not in the assets or processes or systems themselves but rather in the interconnections and the coordinating mechanisms that enable the most efficient and competitive use of these assets, processes or systems.

Organizational capabilities are a source of competitive advantage because they are unique to the firm, often invisible or opaque to outsiders, and therefore difficult for competitors to imitate; they are socially complex and deeply embedded in the firm.[133] Social complexity reflects the fact that capabilities are based on the social interactions between employees within an organization. For example, the unique ways in which a team approaches and solves problems and faces challenges in one firm will be different from the ways in which teams do so in other firms. Socially complex capabilities lack an identifiable owner in an organization and do not reside in an individual who can be hired away by competitors. For similar reasons, a competitor with deep pockets cannot buy a firm's unique socially complex and embedded capabilities[134] unless the entire firm is acquired or merges with another. Thus, even though K-Mart hired several of Wal-Mart's senior managers, it could not replicate Wal-Mart's legendary logistics capability.

Organizational capabilities that can generate a competitive advantage for a firm are often invisible, that is, it is not evident to competitors exactly how the firm combines various assets and systems to develop the capabilities. The capabilities are also based on tacit learning,[135] that is, learning that happens through interactions within the organization rather than via formal training or education programs. Some scholars use the term causally ambiguous[136] to indicate that competitors, outsiders, and sometimes even the firm's own employees are not only not sure how the capabilities are developed but are not sure how these capabilities lead to superior performance. This makes the capabilities difficult to identify and imitate by competitors. These capabilities are competitively valuable because they are not easily replicated.

The most valuable capabilities are path dependent upon a combination of unique organizational actions and learning undertaken over a period of time.[137] Some scholars argue that luck plays a part in developing these capabilities, that is, idiosyncratic decisions that the firm made in the past that somehow or accidentally created a strategic fit with unexpected changes in the business environment.[138] The capabilities that enable a firm to successfully adapt to and manage a change in the business's external environment also enable it to manage different types of change including evolving societal demands for sustainability. Hence, capabilities are capable of multiple uses, for example, product or business model innovation for reducing environmental footprint while improving customer value at the same time. These capabilities may reside in the interconnections between several different functions and levels within an organization.

Critical capabilities for sustainable innovation

A firm's rate of innovation is an important determinant of its profitability. Above industry-average profits are generated because innovations enable a longer revenue-generating time-horizon and the potential to acquire a dominant share of the market. Furthermore, radical and disruptive innovations are important determinants of future profitability and competitive advantage. Radical innovations are those that make a significant improvement in performance or a significant shift from existing performance by solving a complex problem that existing products don't solve. Hence, radical innovations make quantum leaps in their industry and create new product categories (such as the iPod and iPad) and require longer competitor response time, thus allowing the firm to capture monopoly profits (or "rents" as they are known in economics jargon). In contrast to radical innovations, disruptive innovations often emerge by offering inferior performance to current customers but meet the needs of an unserved or under-served market. They gradually improve in performance, and eventually disrupt the industry. Examples are the PC's disruption of the mainframe computer, the digital camera's disruption of photo films and film-based cameras, and the mini steel mills' disruption of large steel mills. Therefore, the potential for an increased rate of radical innovation or a disruptive innovation is a key to long-term competitive advantage. Such innovations require the firm to stay ahead of competitors in identifying opportunities and trends relevant to its industry and its customers' needs. Hence, in order for sustainable business innovations to generate competitive advantage, they need to be radical and/or disruptive, requiring longer response time from competitors.

Radical and disruptive *sustainable* products, technologies, and business models require the managers of the firm to understand the sustainability challenges as they evolve in social consciousness and how these challenges affect their firm and how their firm's operations affect these challenges. For example, Coca-Cola has realized that the main sustainability challenge faced by their firm is clean water. Coca-Cola's operations use large quantities of water in their products and in the production process. At the same time, its operations have major negative impacts on scarce clean water available for human and animal consumption, agriculture, and other uses. The other major sustainability challenge that Coca-Cola has identified is packaging material used for its products in terms of the raw materials (plastics and aluminum) used and the solid waste created after use. In order to tackle their interface with the big sustainability challenges of clean water and packaging-based solid waste, Coca-Cola had to understand the dimensions of the problem by generation of new information from stakeholders affected by the corporation's operations, combining this new knowledge in unique ways to identify innovations that have the potential to create economic, social, and environmental value, and the execution of these innovations successfully in markets. One of these innovations is the "plant bottle" that uses 30 percent plant-based material rather than the previous 100 percent petroleum-based plastics.

Hence, the capabilities that are important for enabling innovation of sustainable processes, products, services, and business models involve organizational processes, systems, and routines to acquire new external information, to generate learning and knowledge combinations within the organization, and to generate a continuous stream of innovations. These capabilities are valuable not only for sustainable innovations, but for enabling a firm to adapt to, and compete, in turbulent and rapidly changing environments that they face currently and will continue to face in the future. These three critical capabilities are depicted in Figure 6.1.

Figure 6.1 **Critical capabilities for sustainable innovation**

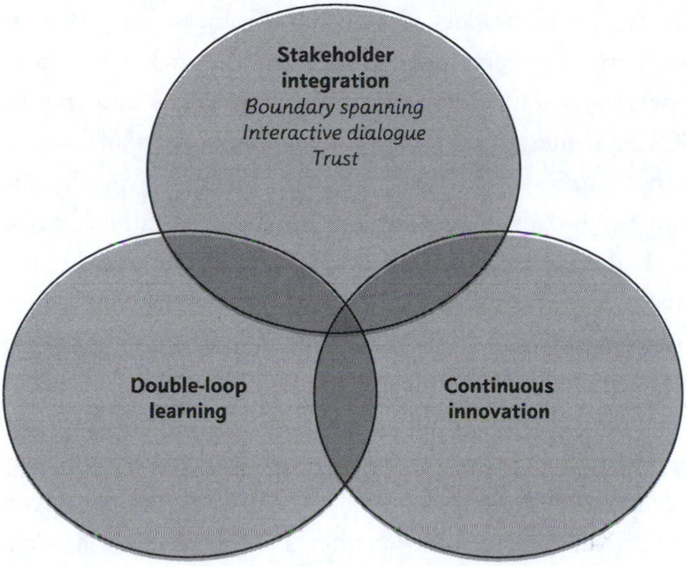

Capability for stakeholder integration

The importance of stakeholders

Stakeholders are the firm's windows to evolving societal concerns. A stakeholder is "any group or individual who can affect or is affected by the achievement of an organization's purpose."[139] Depending upon the specific concerns that a stakeholder group may have about the various impacts of the firm's operations, it may focus on economic, social, or environmental issues, or a combination of them. For example, stakeholder concerns may range from economic issues such as shareholder returns in terms of dividends and capital appreciation, jobs created by the firm, and tax revenues generated; to social issues such as preservation of community culture and heritage, fair wages, fair prices, distribution of income, and diversity; to environmental issues such as preserving ecosystems, clean water, clean air, and reducing carbon footprint.

The stakeholders may be visible to the firm in its operating environment. Such stakeholders include shareholders, investors, employees, customers, suppliers, media, local communities within which the firm's operations are located, regulators, and social and environmental NGOs that interact with the company on a regular basis. On the other hand, some stakeholders may be invisible to the firm because they may be global or distant. In the Nike example discussed in Chapter 2, the concerns over working conditions and living wages in sweatshops run by Nike's subcontractors began with an NGO in Indonesia, spread to NGOs in the US, and then spread to college campuses across the US. Similarly, in the case of the disposal of Shell UK's *Brent Spar* offshore oil platform, stakeholder concerns began to escalate when Greenpeace Germany took Shell UK by surprise when they boarded the oil platform. Shell UK did not consider Greenpeace Germany its stakeholder (see Chapter 2 for a discussion) since Germany does not have access to the North Sea and does not have offshore oil rigs. Until the 2013 collapse of the Rana Plaza building in Dacca, Bangladesh, killed over a thousand workers, NGO concerns and protests over the working conditions and safety of these workers was off the radar of well-known global clothing brands.

Societal understanding of sustainability challenges is continuously evolving. Correspondingly, societal demands about which sustainability challenges business should address have also evolved during the past five decades. During the 1960s and 1970s, societal focus was on highly visible challenges such as cleaning up of noxious emissions and wastes from smokestacks or from effluent pipes, and the safety of employees in the workplace. However, in the 2000s the focus shifted toward much more complex challenges such as climate change, ecosystem biodiversity, fair trade, human rights, and poverty. As explained in earlier chapters, firms often have global supply chains and hence have multiple social and environmental impacts, via suppliers, distributors, retailers, and consumers spread over several countries. Changes in societal expectations of sustainability challenges and how business impacts affect society increasingly create a business environment that is not only complex but also dynamic (continuously changing) in terms of knowledge required, technologies, issue dimensions, and potential solutions. Thus, the knowledge that a firm requires to address sustainability challenges is not only complex and dynamic, but it transcends organizational boundaries and requires the engagement of multiple external groups (stakeholders) wherein this evolving knowledge resides.

Stakeholders as a source of learning

Stakeholders impacted by a firm's operations expect that the firm should undertake timely strategic changes to address their concerns. At the same time, knowledge about the dimensions of sustainability challenges and potential solutions to manage these challenges is constructed in real time via interactions with various stakeholders. As in the case of Nike, the *Brent Spar*, and Monsanto examples discussed previously, lack of timely response by the firm to stakeholder demands may lead to the rapid formation of stakeholder swarms that can seriously affect a firm's reputation among its customers and in the media.

Since knowledge about sustainability challenges among stakeholders is dynamic and complex, in order for a firm to develop effective solutions, it needs to find ways to tap this evolving knowledge of social and environmental issues and emerging technologies. Solutions emerge from collective intelligence rather than from the firm's expertise alone. Managers also need to understand that sustainable value generated by the firm (economic, social, and environmental value created) is determined as much by its stakeholders as by its managers and the top management team. Shareholders, investors, and employees determine economic value that a firm needs to generate—acceptable returns on investment, equity, and sales; social nongovernmental organizations (NGOs) and local communities determine social value—appropriate living wage of employees of subcontractors, working conditions, and fair prices to farmers of agricultural commodities; and environmental NGOs and regulators determine environmental value—acceptable standards of clean air, clean water, and biodiversity.

Stakeholders also provide valuable and meaningful advice to the firm. Competitors inform and affect a firm's strategy based on the strategies that they adopt; social and environmental NGOs shape public opinion and media reports; industry associations help disseminate best practices and shape public policy; and collaborators provide complementary capabilities that help design sustainable products, services, business models, and technologies.

Stakeholder integration

As societal understanding of global sustainability challenges evolves, the multiple dimensions of challenges such as climate change, and the emerging technologies and business models that may present solutions to these challenges, are too complex for one person or one team in a firm to understand in their entirety. Traditionally firms develop the capability to absorb external information and knowledge from a limited set of external economic stakeholders such as alliance partners, suppliers, and customers. External knowledge for firms generally emerges during economic activities such as acquisitions, purchasing, licensing, contractual agreements, and inter-organizational relationships. As the firm looks for unrelated opportunities to redefine its business, complementary knowledge and overlaps between the external and current firm knowledge are less important than radical new ideas. The sparking of new possibilities becomes an important objective. Therefore, in such instances, past experience with its economic stakeholders should not entirely define the focus of a firm's technological search, and firms should not necessarily seek information in areas in which they have had previous success because they are seeking new environments and business models.[140] In fact, firms need to overcome the liability of past experience and models of inter-actions with its current economic stakeholders (suppliers, investors, partners, and customers) and rather seek to explore information that tempers the relevance and importance of past experience and suc-cess. The exploration is in the form of seeking different perspectives, risk taking, experimentation, discovery, and innovation. The focus of exploration is now the gathering of new information that is broad and general on many different ideas and alternatives rather than ana-lyzing the feasibility of any one alternative or opportunity, as is the focus in stable environments.

Therefore, managers trying to make sense in dynamically complex environments need to foster and develop a community of knowl-edge[141] that consists of all the stakeholders who can inform them on the sustainability challenge rather than just the traditional economic stakeholders (customers, suppliers, and investors) that they deal with regularly as they conduct business. In such a diverse network, it is possible that many stakeholders will not directly meet each other but the connections will create multiple channels for sharing and transfer of knowledge. Within the context of dynamic complexity, the firm needs to extend its scope to include stakeholders along its global value chain and even at the periphery of its operations.[142]

Diverse and distant stakeholders add value in the exploration proc-ess because strong ties that characterize the firm's relationships with suppliers, customers, and alliance partners constrain the gathering of information unrelated to current business provide redundant infor-mation and limit a firm's "openness to information and to alternative ways of doing things, producing forms of collective blindness that sometimes have disastrous effects."[143] On the other hand, weak ties or the lack of ties that characterize stakeholders at the periphery of a firm's operations require low investment in relationships and allow wider reach into divergent perspectives. Moreover, extending and expanding the breadth and depth of knowledge exposure positively influences a firm's propensity to explore new knowledge.

Therefore, in order to build a capacity for sustainable innovation, a firm needs the capability to tap knowledge embedded in stakeholder networks, by establishing trust-based collaborative relationships with a wide variety of stakeholders, especially those with non-economic (social and environmental) goals.[144] This is a capability of integrating stakeholders into the firm's knowledge creation and learning process that will lead to sustainable innovations. Corporate processes are normally developed to integrate primary stakeholders such as customers, suppliers, employees, and shareholders to help improve operations in order to achieve economic goals. While a firm certainly needs to integrate these primary stakeholders (especially employees) into processes to help build understanding of evolving sustainability technologies, science, regulations, products, services, business models, and any other relevant information, it also needs to integrate other (secondary) stakeholders such as local communities, environmental/social NGOs, and regulators, among others to develop an understanding of the sustainability landscape from diverse perspectives. The secondary stakeholders help a firm understand the dimensions of issues that managers are unfamiliar with, such as health and ecosystem impacts of the firm's emissions and effluents, biodiversity impacts of the firm's operations, the carbon cycle, climate change, social justice, living wage and fair prices, and rural poverty.

Building the capability of stakeholder integration requires that the firm embrace both goals: goodwill generation among diverse stakeholder groups to avoid the formation of adversarial swarms; and knowledge generation related to sustainability challenges, potential solutions, and emerging technologies.

The outcome of engaging and integrating the perspectives of multiple stakeholders is not just the accumulation of facts but also the development of managerial self-identities, values, and perspectives on issues that are evolving in a dynamically complex environment, shared learning, and shared sense-making about sustainability via social and collective learning.

Boundary spanning

Extending the knowledge network of the firm involves boundary spanning to identify and map stakeholders who could be instrumental in helping the firm understand the dimensions of sustainability challenges, developing a deep understanding of their concerns, and establishing empathy with their perspectives. A boundary-spanner is any manager or employee who interacts regularly with the firm's external constituents. Under conditions of dynamic complexity, when it is not clear what information is relevant and where to look for information, a centralized department or unit does not provide an effective link to monitor changes in the environment. A firm needs to foster an organic organizational structure that creates a broad range of receptors at its boundaries where managers act as conduits into the firm for a diversity of voices. The boundary-spanners extend the scope of the stakeholder network beyond the core stakeholders to the periphery of the firm by identifying the networks of stakeholders that branch out from the nodes of their primary stakeholders such as suppliers, customers, regulators, local communities, and investors.[145]

Developing a stakeholder integration capability requires that the firm train and sensitize the boundary-spanning managers to suspend disbelief and be open to information that disconfirms the existing mental models and dominant logic in the firm. Effective boundary-spanners should not look for solutions to problems but ask the right questions in order to identify how sustainability challenges affect the short-term and long-term competitiveness and survival of their firm. Looking for solutions to existing problems in context of current products and business models can constrain imagination. For example, when faced with disconfirming information in the form of unusually low ozone readings in the Earth's atmosphere, scientists at NASA assumed that it was a measurement problem and redesigned the measurement system so that it could not record ozone levels that were so low. A review of the original data several years later confirmed that the ozone layer was indeed being depleted and eventually led to a treaty phasing out ozone-depleting chemicals, seven years too late.[146]

In order to be able to identify and channel the relevant information from external stakeholders, especially those that may be adversarial to the firm, boundary-spanners need to empathize with differences between the perspectives of the stakeholders and those of the firm. Empathy begins with training boundary-spanners in the language that various stakeholder groups use to debate complex sustainability issues and the meaning underlying the usage of different terms. For example, in the context of the debate in the US and Canada around the extraction of natural gas from shale rock, the term "fracking" (hydraulic fracturing) is a technical term for the industry signaling progress and profitability, while for environmental groups, farmers, and land users it has connotations of environmental destruction. The shared language and terminology allows a conversation with stakeholders to begin, and information to flow.

Firms are struggling to understand and operationalize the concept of sustainable development in relation to their business. In order to begin absorbing stakeholder perspectives, the boundary-spanners need to be educated in concepts such as carrying capacity, ecological footprint, habitat restoration, species extinction, and so forth. In 1997 Shell Expro (UK) sent its employees to a workshop with facilitators from the Natural Step and the Environment Council to understand the language of sustainability before developing its "Sustainable Development Business Plan" in consultation with stakeholders.[147]

Interactive dialogue

The capability of stakeholder integration requires that the firm create opportunities and forums for interactive dialogue between managers and multiple stakeholders concerned with the preservation of the natural environment and fostering social justice. Firms need to create incentives and training programs to develop managerial abilities to listen to and understand the viewpoints of the stakeholders concerned about sustainability challenges that are relevant to the firm's operations.

As described in Chapter 5, effective performance evaluation systems that create an opportunity frame are designed to reward managers not only for achieving production and financial goals, but also for achieving low levels of stakeholder complaints and high levels of positive feedback from stakeholder groups. Employees are also provided discretion via flexibility in their operating budgets to experiment with different ways of generating positive social and environmental impacts, enabling them to respond quickly to some of the suggestions of external stakeholders, further improving collaborative relationships and mutual trust.

Transparency-based trust

Trust with stakeholders is built around a shared understanding of sustainability challenges such as climate change or fair wages and prices based on shared meaning and shared narratives or stories. Trust leads to shared goals for addressing these challenges and shared values around sustainability problems. Diversity in the types of stakeholders that the firm interacts with ensures the absence of groupthink or collective blindness leading to new configurations of knowledge. Trust creates social capital between the firm and external constituents, encouraging cooperative behavior. Thus, trust-based interactions with stakeholders allow a firm to tap into its broader stakeholder networks, enhance the breadth of knowledge and perspectives on a problem domain, and generate novel insights and perspectives. Trust-based relationships with stakeholders also provide the context within which newly created knowledge can be applied, such as in emerging markets at the base of the pyramid.[148]

Trust between the firm and its stakeholders helps anticipate and avoid future conflicts by engendering feelings of procedural justice and commitment. While a diverse stakeholder network provides rich access to information, it is the quality of relationships that enables the full realization of the knowledge creation potential. Trust facilitates the quality of relationships by motivating intense and complex communication processes needed to transfer tacit knowledge between the stakeholder networks and the firm. *Non-economic stakeholders in particular do not have a quantitative benchmark to measure the outcomes of their relationship with the firm and rely on trust for reciprocity rather than exchange of value.* Hence, trust facilitates information exchange by enabling the diffusion of norms of mutual gain, forbearance and reciprocity across the network.

Some stakeholders closer to the firm's operations, such as local communities or regulators, have no incentive or interest in building relational capital or strong social ties with the firm. Stakeholders at the periphery may have even less interest in developing relational capital with the focal firm. Therefore, firms can create the trust required for free exchange of information via a *quid pro quo* based on transparency and openness. Adversarial stakeholders and those at the periphery will not be willing participants in conversations unless they can trust the firm to be transparent about the information they are seeking. As ambiguity prevents stakeholders from verifying that the firm actually behaves as it says it does, transparency is critical to maintaining commitment to future information exchange and helps draw in stakeholders that are increasingly further away from the core into the conversation. Hence, trust is achieved both via interactions between stakeholders and the firm's boundary-spanners and via transparent corporate reporting systems. To facilitate transparency, organizational information that may be relevant, important, and interesting for stakeholders needs to be made available to the boundary-spanners. Information availability will also enable boundary-spanners to correct any misconceptions and false or incomplete information that stakeholders may have.

Firms can get better at boundary spanning and generating knowledge from stakeholder interactions as they gain more experience, making them attractive to engage as partners for stakeholders increasingly further away from the firm's core operations. Increased experience also reduces internal barriers to stakeholder engagement by providing information on the likely behavior of other stakeholders, alleviating risk, and enhancing willingness to form linkages.

Benefits

Integrating varied and multiple stakeholder voices into strategic decision-making can potentially alter organizational knowledge structures. The potential for learning in such diverse information contexts is higher when the firm faces an ambiguous environment because the knowledge in a stakeholder network is much greater than collectively within the firm or in any individual stakeholder group. A firm's communities of interaction are effective at helping its managers in generating, amplifying, transferring, and recombining knowledge.[149] Through stakeholder information exchanges, it is possible for a firm to appreciate and understand the possibilities for action in balancing conflicting stakeholder influences to anticipate and strategize for managing dynamically complex sustainability issues. As external issues evolve and are socially constructed, continued and complex social interactions between a firm and its stakeholders lead to ongoing learning and knowledge development.

These close interactions increase the likelihood that the representatives of stakeholder groups have positive and favorable influences on critical decisions made by these groups in respect of the firm. For example, regulators may give the benefit of the doubt in case of minor infractions to companies that are perceived as sincere because they normally comply or go beyond compliance with regulations. Regulators focus more on firms that tend to have a pattern of noncompliance toward social and environmental standards. This translates into a greater license to operate. Other benefits for the firm include an improved corporate reputation that translates into favorable economic transactions and increased goodwill. A higher license to operate allows for an easier and faster passage through public consultation hearings and approval processes for new developments. As discussed in Chapter 3, faster project approvals lead to savings in project cost overruns, lower interest charges, and lower litigation expenses.

Chapter 5 described how a firm can foster an opportunity frame to create incentives for managers to view sustainability challenges as opportunities rather than as threats and to view them as positive sources of gain rather than loss, that are controllable. Similarly, trust-based stakeholder relationships help create external positive reinforcement and support for sustainable solutions, help managers develop business logic and a business case for tackling sustainability challenges, and a flow of ideas and information to resolve uncertainty and ambiguity around the sustainability challenges.

The trust and credibility developed by proactive companies with a variety of stakeholder groups is a path-dependent strategic capability that cannot be easily imitated by competitors. This capability is an asset, based upon a pattern of consistent actions by the companies to generate positive social and environmental performance in consultation with a diversity of stakeholder groups. This capability is firm-specific because it is based on fundamental changes in business ideology and values accompanied by changes in organizational design over a long period of time. This capability is socially complex since it resides within the interactions between the firm's employees by virtue of the corporate culture. At the same time, this capability is also externally socially complex because it relies on collaborative trust-based relationships between boundary-spanners and external stakeholders. Hence, this is a competitively valuable capability that cannot be easily acquired or copied by competitors.

Capability for double-loop organizational learning

The information acquired by managers as a result of stakeholder integration needs to be converted into knowledge that can enable the emergence of innovative products, services, and business models to address negative sustainability impacts of business operations.

Conversion of information into knowledge requires a capability for higher-order or double-loop learning. Single-loop learning involves the detection and correction of error. Under single loop learning, existing goals and rules are not questioned and managers take goals, values, frameworks, and, to a significant extent, existing strategies for granted. Double-loop learning requires cognitive stress (see Chapter 5) to overcome the managerial tendency to make decisions on autopilot, which lead to biased outcomes. Cognitive stress may lead to the questioning of the goals themselves and the processes, actions, rules, and routines that managers normally follow to achieve the goals. Such double-loop learning leads to a re-evaluation of strategy.[150]

While decision-making under single-loop learning is often routine and automatic, under double-loop learning the basic assumptions behind ideas or policies are confronted and hypotheses are tested,[151] leading to changed world-views. The outcomes are:

- Changed business models based on customer utility delivered. For example, Interface's change of focus from selling carpets to leasing floor comfort, or New England Electric's change of focus toward providing energy and climate comfort rather than electricity, or Dofasco's focus on structural strength rather than steel that led to the manufacture of ultra-light steels based on composite materials

- Changed business models that substitute services for material products and virtual organizational forms for physical operations. These include cost-efficient, distributed, sustainable technologies for delivering consumer value digitally instead of centralized high-cost operations that require extensive distribution across long distances

- Disruptive innovations in emerging markets to meet the unmet needs of marginalized segments of society

Positioning themselves at the intersection of different perspectives allows managers to see new combinations of ideas with greater ease.

A diverse stakeholder interface creates a rich space for learning by changing the social context of knowledge, the mental context of the problem, and often the physical context that takes managers out of the organizational setting where traditional mental models prevail. Just as immersion in a different culture allows managers to better understand the appropriate business systems, processes, and product/service modifications in international markets, spending time in homeless shelters, within rural areas in developing countries, or in areas where nature has been depleted or devastated provides a radically different physical and mental context to spark contextual sense-making around sustainability challenges.

It has been found that the mere presence of representatives from minorities in a group or on the board of directors of an organization[152] helps provide unique perspectives on strategic issues and challenges the conventional wisdom among board members by prompting divergent thinking among majority directors. Therefore, radical perspectives from the periphery of stakeholder groups has an even greater potential for generating learning that can lead to knowledge for radical and disruptive sustainable innovation.[153]

Knowledge in the form of insights, interpretation, and information from diverse stakeholders, especially those with unconventional and disconfirming views about the firm's business, can potentially challenge managers' fundamental business models and frames of reference. When managers encounter views and ideas that disconfirm their frames of reference about sustainability issues, such as the role of business in preserving ecosystem biodiversity or in addressing third-world poverty, they are forced to make sense of views that appear incompatible with conventional business thinking. Such sense-making, as discussed in Chapter 5, generates cognitive stress and forces managers to look for new interpretations of existing problems. Such sense-making also catalyzes double-loop learning.[154]

Complex learning flows from the challenges that managers face in trying to balance conflicting economic, social, and ecological stakeholder demands. Addressing such challenges creates cognitive stress-based learning that is unique as compared to learning generated through interacting solely with economic stakeholders such as suppliers, customers, and investors. Hence, a firm's unique configuration of stakeholder influences, networks, and relationships has the potential to generate double-loop learning processes that change managerial world-views about business models and products. More importantly, a holistic world-view about a firm's business environment has the potential to create an imagination about future strategic competitive positions and can spark a Schumpeterian process of creative destruction.[155] Such higher-order learning or double-loop learning capability is unique and inimitable due to the socially complex embedding in the interactions between a firm's employees and between a firm's employees and its unique configuration of stakeholders.

A capability for organizational learning enables a continuous flow of competitively useful knowledge, enabling the firm to maintain a dynamic alignment of its strategy with the changing environment. Such knowledge flows signal to the firm the investments it should make in appropriate tangible and intangible organization-specific resources and capabilities to generate new value-creating strategies.

Collaborative influences from economic stakeholders such as other business units, suppliers, customers, and alliance partners will generate knowledge that helps the firm improve operating efficiencies and existing products, design products for the environment, and analyze product life-cycles.[156] At the same time, it is also important for the firm to develop learning processes that will develop a competitive imagination for future sustainable business models and products.[157] By doing so, firms may be able to develop knowledge about unmet needs and about evolving technological, political, social, and environmental trends from stakeholders who may have no incentive or interest in collaborative and social interactions with the firm.

A firm with the capabilities of stakeholder integration and double-loop learning is able to balance and integrate the conflicting interests and goals of economic and non-economic stakeholders while generating learning that allows it to gather dispersed and evolving external knowledge from stakeholder networks. Hence the two capabilities reinforce and complement each other. Ultimately stakeholders want to see outcomes in the form of resource deployments, commitments, and transparency of information in response to their concerns. In order to respond to stakeholder concerns, firms need a capability for continuous innovation that ensures that the firm is generating a series of innovations in practices, processes, products, and even business models in response to stakeholder concerns to address sustainability challenges and generate competitive advantage in the long term.

Capability for continuous innovation

A firm's rate of innovation is an important determinant of its profitability. Innovation enables the firm to generate profits consistently above industry average due to a longer revenue time-horizon and the potential to acquire a dominant share of the market. More radical innovations require longer competitor response time, thus allowing the firm to capture monopoly profits for a longer period. Therefore, the potential for an increased rate of radical or disruptive innovation is a key to competitive advantage. Disruptive innovation enables the firm to redefine industries and become first movers by identifying emerging technologies and business models relevant to its customers' needs.

Double-loop learning processes, triggered by a firm's capabilities for stakeholder integration and organizational learning, foster a changing experiential base of organizational activities, routines, and goals. Changes in technologies, processes, specifications, inputs, and products can stimulate the building-up of knowledge-based assets.[158] While innovation provides an opportunity for a firm to be the first mover, the likelihood of a firm benefiting in a sustained manner from first-mover status will depend on the development of a capability for *continuous* innovation. As the window for technological and business model innovations gets ever shorter (as seen over the last decade), even internal innovations in systems and management practices are rarely defensible against competitive actions. However, a capability for continuously generating a stream of innovations enables an organization to stay a step ahead of competitors who do not possess this capability.

Addressing dynamically complex societal challenges as a component of corporate strategy requires balancing seemingly conflicting perspectives and objectives of diverse stakeholders, many of whom demand conflicting performance on social and environmental challenges. Such balancing requires sustainable business logic (Chapter 4) and changing the existing shared mental models among managers by reinterpretation of existing information and developing new understandings of sustainability challenges in the firm's business environment. For example, these challenges have to be viewed not as threats of regulatory hurdles to be averted through costly compliance but as business opportunities for generating new products, services, and business models that can yield future competitive advantage.

Competitive imagination about future products, services, and business models is sparked when the organization attempts to resolve contradictions created by disconfirming information and divergent stakeholder objectives. Hence, this capability requires integration of diverse and disconfirming information and sharing explicit and tacit knowledge within the organization, combining new information with existing organizational memory, and changing the mental models of decision-makers to generate imaginative products and business models that will address the concerns of diverse stakeholder swarms and contribute to future competitive advantage.

As the firm's boundary-spanners bring fresh perspectives on internal business issues via their intense interactions with stakeholders, firms need to build systems to do both: push the new knowledge through the various internal sub-units and create a pull for this knowledge by raising awareness of sustainability challenges in the business environment for internal operating managers. Such connections require overcoming obstacles to adoption of new perspectives including perceptions of issue uncertainty (as discussed in Chapter 5), lack of understanding of complexities embedded in sustainability challenges, and the existence of different thought worlds within the firm.

Mechanisms to overcome these obstacles may include: cross-functional project teams that are provided with a white space within an organization and assigned a time-bound task of addressing a specific sustainability challenge; sustainability education and training to foster a better understanding of how the organization's current operations have negative social and environmental impacts; job rotation; information sharing; benchmarking of innovation performance against indicators developed in a participative manner; incentive and reward systems; and interactions between boundary-spanners and managers responsible for strategic and operational decisions. Divergent thinking requires the fostering of risk-taking and experimentation by managers by permitting them to deviate from their routines. Most corporate control systems achieve the opposite effect by controlling and punishing variation from original goals and targets. For example, for white space experimental innovations at Nike, the company encourages learning via risk-sharing where no single person is credited for successes while no single person assumes the risk of failures.

Continuous innovation is the process by which innovations of sustainable business models, products, and processes emerge as an outcome of integration of external (as a result of stakeholder integration) and internal knowledge (as a result of higher-order organizational learning). It involves the alteration of knowledge as managers integrate conflicting stakeholder claims and multiple decision criteria by combining previously unconnected activities, routines, and business modelor product elements or by developing novel ways of combining existing activities, routines, and elements. It generates knowledge that enables firms to develop products and business models that address problems and concerns that are common for the business and the stakeholders, helps it improve relationships and build trust with stakeholders, and build social capital. Innovation can be in the form of both adapted and new product-market combinations, and new applications from existing processes. Therefore, this capability generates innovations in products, technologies, and business models as managerial world-views about their business are challenged while trying to resolve the complexities of sustainable challenges.

This is a firm-specific capability since the individual managers may not be able to adopt similar stances on experimentation, learning, and knowledge generation in organizations that do not provide a similar context of stakeholder integration, learning, and knowledge integration. This capability is path-dependent, involving a series of unique interactions and an experiential base of organizational activities over a period of time.

Building sustainable capabilities via collaborations

While organization-specific and socially complex capabilities built over a period of time that are path-dependent on the firm's unique strategies, actions, and history are the most difficult to identify and imitate by competitors, the firm can also build or acquire capabilities via collaborations and alliances. The value of these capabilities depends on how well the acquired capabilities are integrated and embedded within organizational routines and managerial decision-making processes. There are four dominant inter-organizational types of collaborations focused on sustainable innovation:

1. Strategic alliances (i.e., collaborations between firms)

2. Alliances between the firm and an NGO

3. Alliances between the firm and government agencies

4. Alliances between the firm and a university or between an industry association (of which the firm is a member) and a university[159]

The traditional focus of strategic alliances has been on enabling the collaborating firms to meet their strategic economic, financial or market objectives. Increasingly strategic alliances combine economic, social, and environmental objectives involving suppliers, customers, and competitors.[160] Some alliances are focused on bringing together technological capabilities to create environmentally sustainable products and seek new market opportunities, for example, the General Motors–Dow Chemicals partnership to develop commercial hydrogen fuel cells for power generation.[161]

Collaborations between firms and NGOs are often undertaken in order to increase the legitimacy of a firm's products and operations, including endorsement of a firm's products by an NGO via licensing agreements, and sponsorship of core activities or projects of NGOs by firms. However, such collaborations are also undertaken for the transfer of knowledge and capabilities. A famous pioneering corporate–NGO partnership was undertaken in 1990 between McDonald's and the Environmental Defense Fund (EDF). At that time, there was growing public concern over the mountains of non-recyclable packaging—usually polystyrene foam—used by the fast food industry. McDonald's, as the industry leader, faced the greatest public pressure to eliminate its visible waste in the form of polystyrene foam clamshells. The partnership set up a joint project team to analyze McDonald's US operations, including restaurants, distribution centers, and suppliers, to reduce materials used at source; to recycle and re-use materials throughout its supply chain; and to compost organic materials. Even though the project team began with a focus on visible polystyrene foam packaging, it quickly discovered that 80 percent of McDonald's waste was generated behind the counter in food preparation and its supply chain.[162] McDonald's project team was able to build strong waste management capabilities as a result of their partnership with the EDF experts. Within a year, in April 1991, McDonald's announced that it was: switching from polystyrene foam clamshells to paper for sandwich packaging, reducing waste between 70 to 90 percent; converting carry-out bags, coffee filters, and Big

Mac wraps to unbleached paper; incorporating 30 percent post-consumer recycled content in paper napkins; and asking suppliers to incorporate 35 percent post-consumer recycled content into all corrugated shipping boxes. Over the next decade, McDonald's eliminated more than 300 million pounds of packaging, recycled a million tons of corrugated boxes, and reduced restaurant waste by 30 percent. As a result of the packaging changes, McDonald's began to save around $6 million per year.[163]

The partnership was so successful that, in 2003, McDonald's drew on the capabilities of EDF to create a new purchasing policy to reduce the use of antibiotics in poultry production. The new policy reduced nearly 18,000 pounds of antibiotics used by McDonald's poultry suppliers annually. As a result, McDonald's top supplier, Tyson Foods, announced in 2006 that it had cut antibiotic use over 90 percent.[164] This became an industry standard in the fast food industry and, by 2006, the top four poultry producers in the US had eliminated the use of human antibiotics to promote growth in chickens. Since then, EDF has collaborated with several other companies, including Wal-Mart, to reduce the environmental footprint of their operations and the products they sell, and with private equity firms like KKR and the Carlyle Group to improve the environmental performance of the companies they own. This is an important partnership because the private equity sector invests in thousands of small companies (10 percent of the US economy) that do not have the human resources to undertake sustainability innovation on their own.[165] Similarly, Procter & Gamble claims that it has saved almost $1 billion in the past ten years by reducing packaging through its partnerships with environmental NGOs.[166]

Collaborations between firms and government agencies are undertaken to enhance a firm's legitimacy, to manage and influence regulations, and to develop and acquire capabilities. Government agencies play a major role in technology transfer and building environmental management capabilities for small and medium-sized firms. They also play a role in strengthening regional inter-firm environmental networks or clusters.[167] Such collaborations become knowledge repositories for clusters and networks of firms in a geographic region and create forums and networks to foster inter-firm learning and knowledge transfer.

Firms may also acquire capabilities by entering into collaborations with universities for collaborative R&D; providing funds for contract research; enlargement and commercialization of university-developed technology and intellectual property; and employee education in sustainability.[168] For example, in 2008, BP entered into an alliance with the University of California at Berkeley to develop renewable energy solutions.[169]

The potential for collaborations and alliances to build critical capabilities and knowledge to enable sustainable innovation depends on finding the right partners. The firm needs to carefully screen, assess, and select partners based on the capabilities, technologies, and access that they will bring, the complementarity of the goals of the partner with the firm's goals, and commonality of sustainability values. In managing these alliances and collaborations, it is important to develop the most appropriate governance structure. This may range from informal knowledge-sharing on specific social or environmental issues to formalized joint R & D and product development such as the partnership between GM and Dow Chemicals or between Greenpeace and Foron Household Appliances in Germany during 1992–93 for the development and marketing of a low environmental footprint refrigerator.[170] The partners bring different strategic goals and motivations, different cultures, and different organizational systems to the collaboration. Therefore, the governance structure must balance this diversity and channel it toward capability building and sustainable innovation. For example, investor-owned firms with a profit objective have to be sensitive to the social and environmental objectives of member-owned NGOs. The partners have to be open to advice and ideas from each other, maintain open communication lines, and retain some level of independence for continued success.

Summary

Even if a firm's managers have the motivations, an opportunity frame, and a clearly developed business logic for sustainable innovation, they still need the capacity to implement the innovation process. This capacity is based on three critical capabilities of stakeholder integration, organizational learning, and continuous innovation. The three capabilities complement and reinforce each other. A firm without all three is likely to struggle to compete in a sustainable world. The knowledge required to tackle global sustainability challenges transcends the firm's boundaries and is complex and dynamic. A capability for stakeholder integration helps firms gather information and build a knowledge base that enables them to understand the dimensions of the challenge. This capability requires boundary spanning, interactive dialogue, and building trust. This information is combined with the firm's existing knowledge structures to generate double-loop organizational learning that enables managers to challenge existing mental models and frames of reference. Finally, firms need to close the loop because, in order to build a capability for stakeholder integration, firms need to generate a stream of continuous sustainable innovations that signal to the stakeholders that they should continue to engage with the firm. These capabilities are competitively valuable only if they are inimitable because they are socially complex, organization-specific, and path-dependent on the unique history, strategy, and actions of a firm. However, in a dynamic and complex business environment, firms also need to acquire some capabilities through collaborations and alliances with other firms, NGOs, governments, and universities. While it is important to structure and govern all alliances appropriately, alliances with sustainable objectives must be based on shared social and environmental values and goals.

When firms enter radically different contexts and markets such as the base of the pyramid (BOP) where people have unmet needs but do not have the capacity to pay for conventional products and services, firms need to co-create (with communities and consumers in the BOP) sustainable innovations that are radical and disruptive. While firms in the developed world may be able to compete in the short term with a limited set of capabilities, in a BOP context characterized by major social and environmental challenges, firms need not only different strategies but transformational capabilities that integrate knowledge not from core stakeholders, as discussed in this chapter, but rather from those at the fringe of their networks. This is discussed in Chapter 7.

Seven
Sustainable innovation at the base of the pyramid

It was the best of times, it was the worst of times, it was the age of wisdom, it was the age of foolishness, it was the epoch of belief, it was the epoch of incredulity, it was the season of Light, it was the season of Darkness, it was the spring of hope, it was the winter of despair, we had everything before us, we had nothing before us, we were all going direct to heaven, we were all going direct the other way—in short, the period was so far like the present period, that some of its noisiest authorities insisted on its being received, for good or for evil, in the superlative degree of comparison only.

Charles Dickens, *A Tale of Two Cities*

The World Commission on Environment and Development (WCED) in its report *Our Common Future* coined the often cited definition of sustainable development as the "development that meets the needs of the present without compromising the ability of future generations to meet their own needs" (p. 43). This definition highlights two key concepts: the concept of meeting the needs of humanity, particularly the essential needs of the world's poor, to which overriding priority should be given; and the importance of paying equal attention not only to present but also future needs.

In 2002, C.K. Prahalad and Stuart Hart wrote a pioneering article titled "The Fortune at the Bottom of the Pyramid," which made a business case for the development of radically different business models that addressed the markets at the bottom of the income pyramid (BOP).[171] They argued that BOP markets were radically different from middle-income and high-income markets on four dimensions:

- The consumers in these markets have severely limited access to capital, to the extent that even buying a bottle of shampoo may represent a major investment

- A distribution infrastructure does not exist or is deficient, in the form of paved roads, transportation, and telecommunications

- Gross margins per item are very small because the price point has to be affordable for the consumers with an income that may range from a dollar a day up to three dollars a day

- The size of the market is large. It is estimated that there are around four billion people who live on less than $2.50 a day in BOP markets.[172] The unit sales can be potentially large albeit with small gross margins, resulting in large absolute sales and profits

Several different approaches to developing successful strategies for doing business in BOP markets have been recommended. Some authors have advocated selling traditional products with reduced and limited features at margins that are significantly higher than middle-income markets. The argument made is that the poor obtain loans at usurious rates from moneylenders—as much as 53 times those paid by middle- and upper-income consumers, at 600 to 1000 percent versus 12 to 18 percent bank lending rates; or buy water from private operators for $1.12 per cubic meter versus $0.03 per cubic meter for the municipal supply, because the poor often do not have water connections. Therefore, this perspective proposes that firms can provide products and services at high margins and this would not only benefit the poor but also generate large profits (and thus, result in a "fortune at the bottom of the pyramid" for the selling firm).[173]

Indeed, early BOP business models included sachet-sized packs of shampoo, tiny soaps, and tiny detergent cakes sold by Unilever's Indian subsidiary Hindustan Unilever Ltd. (HUL) to the poor. These small packs were affordable as a single unit but represented a very high price per liter or ounce when compared to normal-sized shampoos and soaps. These small packs resulted in large quantities of packaging waste that littered the environment and also substituted oil-based washing powders traditionally used by the poor with phosphate-based detergents that contaminated water bodies and drinking water sources.

Another perspective has argued that profitable BOP models require a 30 percent market penetration in a BOP market, which is very difficult to obtain for individual firms.[174] Some approaches have advocated bundling products, adding functionalities, and adding enabling services to generate higher sales and margins.[175] Others argue that selling consumer products in small packages or services at high margins does not help the poor; rather, the path toward sustainable development for these markets is to integrate the poor at the BOP as suppliers to corporations rather than as customers for products of multinationals.[176] In response, some multinational enterprises attempted to develop supply chains with the poor as suppliers of basic commodities and simple products. However, such business models have not led to significant improvement in critical unmet needs at the BOP such as clean water, affordable energy, hygiene, communications, education, etc. and have not significantly reduced environmental damage.

Successful business models that have generated positive economic, social, and environmental benefits—such as distributed solar lighting, healthcare, and clean water—have often been financially viable only due to subsidies from governments or international bodies such as the

World Health Organization. Success in the BOP requires patient long-term continuous investment in local knowledge and relationships. Some refer to these as native capabilities of becoming indigenous, flying under the radar, and working with non-traditional partners.[177]

In order to develop meaningful approaches to building sustainable business models at the BOP that generate positive social and environmental impacts, a series of meetings were convened by Stuart Hart and hosted by the S.C. Johnson Co. at the Wingspread Conference Center in Racine, Wisconsin. At these meetings, a group of experts from industry, academia, and NGOs developed a BOP protocol that focused on the co-creation of business models by the multinational enterprise based on deep dialogue with consumers at the BOP in order to address genuine unmet needs.[178] The protocol emphasizes embedding of managers in the BOP context, deep listening, and co-creation of products, services, and business models with the local communities and stakeholders within these communities.

This approach requires a holistic integration of the critical capabilities discussed in Chapter 6 into a seamless mega-capability that Stuart Hart and I[179] termed radical transactiveness. This capability enables a firm to develop a process of engagement and innovation for the BOP. This approach also informed the BOP Protocol development process.[180] This integrative capability is especially relevant for sustainable innovation in highly unfamiliar contexts such as BOP[181] markets that are radically different from existing high- and middle-income markets with which most firms are familiar.

A means for successfully implementing sustainable business models at the BOP may require, in some contexts, a strategic bridging approach that enables the creation of a business model including diverse stakeholders who are unwilling to work together. The bridging organization creates a domain around a holistic understanding of common sustainability challenges and goals that various stakeholders can connect with.[182] This chapter draws upon these two concepts—radical transactiveness and strategic bridging—to illustrate how successful sustainable models can be developed in BOP contexts.

Radical transactiveness

The terms "radical" and "transactiveness" are relevant concepts for developing sustainable business models at the BOP. "Radical" represents a focus on stakeholders, previously considered irrelevant or at the fringe of a firm's stakeholder networks that need to be engaged in order to generate competitive imagination for sustainable innovation. "Transactiveness" represents a two-way dialogue with stakeholders for co-creation of sustainable business products and ideas. This capability is broader than the capability of stakeholder integration discussed in Chapter 6 because:

1. It is radical in going beyond the scope of core stakeholders such as customers, investors, suppliers, employees, local communities, media, and NGOs, that a firm normally engages

2. It involves going beyond engagement and interactive dialogue to embedded deep listening by managers in BOP contexts with the fringe stakeholders

As discussed in Chapter 6, interactions with and among diverse stakeholders that extend the boundaries of the firm offer the possibility for learning and growth that the firm could not envision on its own. In the context of the BOP, engaging stakeholders at the fringe of a firm's networks allows it to understand the complex and evolving issues that may potentially affect the basis of its future competitive advantage.

The concept of fringe stakeholders is distinct from the visible and identifiable core stakeholders normally considered by firms to have a stake in its existing operations.[183] As discussed in Chapter 2, core stakeholders are closely connected to the firm's operations and gain a seat at the discussion table by virtue of their power (e.g., investors, governments, customers, media), legitimacy (e.g., employees, suppliers, customers, governments, investors), or the urgency (e.g., NGOs, regulators, local communities) of their claims.[184] Fringe stakeholders, as their name suggests, are at the fringe of a firm's stakeholder networks or operations. They are usually disconnected from or invisible to the firm, especially in the BOP, because they may be remote rather than close like the local community, weak rather than powerful like regulators, poor unlike investors and shareholders, disinterested unlike the media, isolated unlike organized employees or customer groups, non-legitimate with no legal basis to their stake, or even non-human such as animal and plant species damaged or destroyed by a firm's operations. They may be affected by the firm but have little, if any, direct connection to the firm's current activities. However, due to their very nature, the fringe stakeholders may hold perspectives and knowledge radically different from that of the core stakeholders.

For a firm looking to innovate radical and disruptive products and business models to address sustainability challenges in unfamiliar BOP contexts, these perspectives and knowledge may help it identify new idea and opportunities that may become the basis of future competitive advantage. Figure 7.1 depicts the differences between fringe and core stakeholders.

Figure 7.1 **Stakeholders: Core and fringe**

Source: Adapted from S. Hart and S. Sharma, "Radical Transactiveness and Competitive Imagination," *Academy of Management Executive* 17(2) (2003): 56-69.

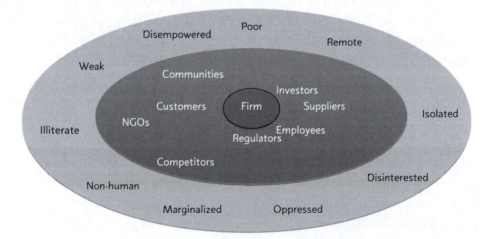

Example: HP Labs—Scaling up innovation at the BOP

Hewlett-Packard's "Living Lab" in the village of Kuppam in India was established in the late 1990s. The objective of this lab was to create an *icommunity* in a small village program to explore business models that would meet the following objectives:

- A sustainable information and communication technology infrastructure

- Self-sustaining new job or income opportunities

- Profitable revenue streams by providing access to new markets

- Appropriate technology innovations and replicable business models

- Leadership and capacity within the local community

- An ecosystem to ensure the broadest possible active inclusion of all the relevant stakeholders in the community

- To learn the potential for information technology and Internet use by the rural poor in developing countries[185]

This was intended to help HP imagine and design the products, services, and business models of the future.[186]

The first initiative for HP in the form of communication kiosks for pay per use by the poor was not successful because local competitors were able to quickly develop lower-cost business models of Internet communication kiosks in India. However, during this embedded deep engagement and listening with fringe stakeholders, the firm gained an in-depth knowledge of the unmet needs of the poor in the Indian BOP market. That knowledge led to a unique business model in which HP Labs India set up grassroots entrepreneurs in small towns and villages for the authentication of legal documents and certificates using state-issued prepaid legal bar codes to substitute for stamped (duty paid) legal paper that was hard to obtain by ordinary citizens in a bureaucratic and corrupt court system. This model was based on the innovation of a proprietary technology in most regular HP printers and based on prepaying stamp duties for legal documentation centrally to the government. HP Labs India developed a Document Authentication System (DAS) that authenticated legal documents and certificates such as educational transcripts, driver's licenses, and citizens' ID cards to overcome fraud and forgery using a two-dimensional barcode in a networked environment. The document can be read using commonly available scanners. The scanned document can be sent to the DAS system over a network which generates a report stating the validity of the document. The DAS protects the privacy of the end-users whose documents are being verified.[187] This innovation quickly traveled up the income pyramid into applications in the middle-income and high-income markets. Some applications include the healthcare industry where all patient documents can be barcoded for easy access and viewing; the automobile industry that uses the barcodes for labels; shipping firms for routing labels; and utilities, banks, and insurance companies that can add a client barcode on all correspondence and contracts.

Knowledge and learning emerging from the capability of radical transactiveness signal to the firm the investments it should make in appropriate resources and capabilities, allowing it to generate new value-creating sustainable business models. For example, Hindustan Unilever Limited (HUL; Unilever's Indian subsidiary, formerly known as HLL or Hindustan Lever Ltd.) requires its managers to spend six weeks living in rural areas to generate knowledge about the hygiene needs and practices of the rural poor. This knowledge has resulted in new product ideas such as a combined soap and shampoo bar, and promotional programs such as street theater, for rural markets. These innovations have also been adopted by Unilever subsidiaries in Brazil and other developing countries.

By drawing on knowledge, perspectives, concerns, and needs of diverse and distant stakeholder groups, radical transactiveness (RT) also helps a multinational or a foreign firm overcome its liability of foreignness by improving relationships and building a fund of goodwill at the grassroots in a BOP market. This not only avoids conflicts and obstacles to operations but also enhances the firm's legitimacy and enables it to engage further in meaningful deep dialogue with stakeholders at the fringe. A major reason for the inability of Coca-Cola to manage the escalating opposition to its operations from farmers in India in 2004 and 2005 over alleged contamination of water sources and depletion of water tables was due to its inability to recognize these farmers as stakeholders. Since the corporation was unable to engage stakeholders at the fringe and focused on its core stakeholders (the government, consumers, investors, and suppliers), the issue was rapidly taken up by Indian NGOs, state and federal governments, international NGOs, students across the US, and finally US consumers, resulting in boycotts of Coca-Cola products across campuses in the US.[188] The situation reached a crisis when the Indian Supreme Court passed a judgment requiring the corporation to hand over its secret formula to the government. Only an intervention by the WWF persuaded the Indian government to withdraw this order.[189]

As a mega-capability, RT consists of two sub-capabilities: the ability to extend the scope of the firm (fan-out); and the ability to integrate diverse and disconfirming knowledge (fan-in). Figure 7.2 illustrates this capability.

Figure 7.2 **Radical transactiveness**

Source: Adapted from S. Hart and S. Sharma, "Radical Transactiveness and Competitive Imagination," *Academy of Management Executive* 17(2) (2003): 56-69.

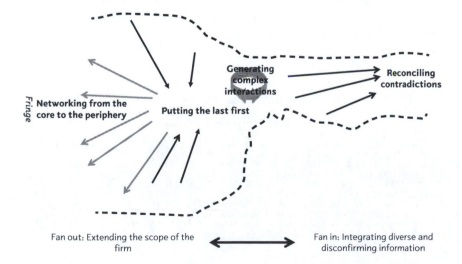

Fan-out sub-capability: Extending the scope of the firm

Identifying and creating an imagination of future sources of competitive advantage via sustainable innovations requires divergent thinking by managers. The BOP markets are so different from the traditional middle- and upper-income markets, with which managers are familiar, that divergent thinking is necessary to identify the unmet needs of both existing customers and those in new unserved markets, and to envision new, disruptive technologies and business models that enable the firm to deliver functionality to existing and new consumers faster, better or more cheaply than competitors. As discussed earlier, in Chapter 6, knowledge that can inform such innovation is not only constantly evolving but is also widely dispersed outside the firm within stakeholder groups that may be neither important, salient, nor situated centrally in a firm's network. As the HP and HUL examples show, these stakeholders are often at the unseen periphery (fringe) of the firm's stakeholder network, such as the urban homeless, the rural poor in developing countries, or even non-human (e.g., endangered) species and nature.[190] The ability to include distant voices from the fringe of an organization's stakeholder network enables a holistic and panoramic view of a firm's changing external environment. This helps the firm understand concerns of distant stakeholders affected indirectly via its upstream supply chain or downstream disposal of its spent products. There are two primary processes for fanning out or extending the scope of the firm: networking from the core to the periphery, and putting the last first.

Networking from the core to the periphery

By identifying parties immediately beyond the core of salient stakeholders (that is, those that are powerful and legitimate with urgent claims), firms can follow the networks of each of these stakeholders in turn to the periphery. For example, when Shell-UK plc decided to dispose of its *Brent Spar* oil drilling platform in the North Sea, it consulted with a wide variety of stakeholders in the UK (including

Greenpeace UK). However, it was forced to abandon its plan under pressure from Greenpeace Germany, which was not considered a stakeholder at the time of the initial decision. By looking at Greenpeace UK's stakeholder network, Shell UK could have potentially identified Greenpeace Germany as a concerned stakeholder and the pressure it could bring to bear on other German stakeholders such as the church, trade unions, small businesses, and finally the German government, which formally voiced its objections to the British government.[191]

Another telling example is that of Monsanto. Between 1993 and 1998, Monsanto spun off its chemicals business and made $8 billion worth of acquisitions in the area of agricultural biotechnology. Through its aggressive promotion of genetically modified (GM) seeds in the US and planting nearly 50 million acres by 1998, the company increased earnings at a compound annual rate of 15.5 percent and grew total return to shareholders 285 percent. Monsanto appeared to have successfully transformed itself from a low-margin producer of chemicals into a technology company with a P/E ratio to match.[192] Yet during this period of strategic transformation and growth, questions unanticipated by Monsanto began to emerge about the potential human health side effects and environmental consequences of biotechnology and the genetic engineering of seeds. "Frankenfoods," as genetically engineered foods had come to be known in Europe, were increasingly under attack by consumer groups, retailers, and NGOs. The backlash also began to manifest itself in the developing world. Millions of small farmers in India, for example, protested in the streets against Monsanto, based on fears that the company would force them to pay international prices by enforcing patent ownership of seed sterilization technology. This technology, dubbed the "terminator" by an NGO, would prevent farmers from propagating the seed from their own crops. Similarly, by looking beyond farmers in the United States to the processing and retail facilities they sold to and to the end-consumers that eventually bought from these retail outlets, Monsanto could potentially have identified groups that had concerns about genetically modified foods. The over one thousand deaths of garment workers at the collapse of the Rana Plaza building in Bangladesh in 2013 indicated that the international fashion houses and garment chains did not consider the workers at their subcontractors' factories to be stakeholders. Attention to these fringe stakeholders could have prevented the deterioration of working conditions to the extent that they resulted in such a large numbers of deaths and an international outcry.

It is not possible for a firm to identify every remote fringe stakeholder that can affect its operations, but an ability and a process to continuously network to the periphery, baked into the managerial DNA, will enable the firm to identify and engage such groups as they evolve, before they become alienated, unwilling to interact with the firm, or even militant and activist (as in the examples of Coca-Cola, Monsanto, and Shell).

Developing this sub-capability or process requires the training of boundary-spanners (managers in marketing, procurement, communications, new business development, and facility managers) in life-cycle assessment (LCA) to help them understand how the operations of the firm, its supply chain, and customers create negative environmental impacts such as waste, pollution, and biodiversity, and negative social impacts, such as inequitable wages, poor working conditions, depletion of community economic capacity, and cultural impacts. These boundary-spanners in turn engage core stakeholders including suppliers, customers, distributors, local communities, NGOs, and government agencies to identify further networks of core stakeholders and the possible negative social and environmental impacts of the operations of each stakeholder in the network.

The managers then can follow this network outward via stakeholder engagement and snowballing to identify the remotest stakeholders affected by the firm's supply chain and consumption or disposal of products. A centralized corporate department—such as sustainable development, new business development, or communications—coordinates information from boundary-spanners to develop an ongoing inventory or repository of the firm's core and fringe stake-holder network and the sustainability issues important within the network. A corporate taskforce that includes operating and facility managers develops strategies for communicating with, and address-ing the concerns of, these stakeholders before they connect with media, labor unions, political forces, or other powerful stakeholders that can raise the profile of an issue or concern. Boundary-spanners in the firm will implement these strategies in collaboration with core stakeholders such as suppliers and distributors. Actions may involve changes in products and services, procurement specifications, recy-cling and take-back of products after consumption, improvement in wages and working conditions at contractors' facilities, and the adop-tion of pollution prevention and control practices by suppliers.

The costs of such networking include training, managerial time in terms of research, engagement and coordination, travel, and other forms of operating slack. These costs are more than likely to be outweighed by the potential benefits of preserving corporate repu-tation and operating legitimacy, and avoiding costly project delays that adversarial stakeholder swarms may cause. Stakeholders usu-ally attack large, highly visible firms with corporate reputations and brand images to protect.[193] For such firms that are usually industry leaders in sales and profits, spending a million dollars on reputation preservation and operating legitimacy usually represents less than one-tenth of one percent of revenues, a fraction of what they would normally spend on product and corporate advertising.

Putting the last first

A second sub-capability, routine, or process critical to fanning out is to begin the radical transactiveness at the fringe of the stakeholder networks rather than working out from the core by "putting the last first."[194] This requires a conscious effort to completely reverse the rules of stakeholder saliency[195] by identifying actors who are power-less, non-legitimate, isolated, or disinterested with respect to the focal firm. These are typical stakeholders at the BOP with no incentive to engage with the firm. It is extremely difficult for managers in existing businesses to identify fringe stakeholders such as the rural poor, urban shantytown dwellers, or advocates for nature's rights. However, placing managers in operating contexts that are the opposite of their current context opens them to hearing stakeholder voices from the periphery. Multinational enterprises such as S.C. Johnson, DuPont, Novartis, Baxter, Ingersoll Rand, the Tata Group, among others, and domestic companies operating in middle- and high-income markets in developing countries, have embedded managers in BOP contexts such as the large slums of Kibera in Nairobi (Kenya), Dharavi in Mumbai (India), and villages in Asia, Africa, and Latin America to understand the needs of the BOP consumer.

Either approach of networking from the core to the periphery or putting the last first would have enabled companies such as Shell, Coca-Cola or Monsanto to anticipate the major incidents that damaged their reputations and affected their operations. Fanning out might also have identified creative new strategies for the firms to pursue that might have avoided the problem in the first place and innovations that would create competitive advantage in the future. For example, in the case of Monsanto, consumer groups in Europe were quite vocal about their concerns relating to the uncertain science around the effects of genetically modified foods. Other stakeholder groups on the "fringe" included millions of small farmers in developing countries such as India. Regrettably, Monsanto did not allow these voices from beyond the core of its stakeholder networks to reach decision-makers. Monsanto followed a conventional process of core stakeholder management that included consulting with its immediate customers (farmers), regulators, and consumer groups in the US. Putting the last first might have enabled Monsanto to develop a different business model that met the needs of all its stakeholders.

The greatest problems with agricultural productivity and poverty exist among the millions of small farmers in the BOP. Therefore, it might have been possible for Monsanto to focus product development on improving the nutritional quality, pest resistance, and water tolerance of tropical crops such as cassava, rice, and sweet potatoes, among others, that dominate in the developing world, rather than the incremental productivity improvement of industrial-scale corn, cotton, wheat, and soybean which are dominant in the developed world.

In terms of developing the processes and routines around this subcapability, corporate managers in areas such as sustainability or business development conduct research around issues of climate change, biodiversity, social equity, ecosystem preservation, human rights, etc., and identify stakeholders (even if they are not currently considered stakeholders) who are affected by or concerned about these issues or whose lives could be improved by building business solutions around these issues. These stakeholders are often in jurisdictions that are economically and socially at the opposite end of the spectrum from the current contexts of the firm. It is important to identify and avoid communities and cultures that are functioning sustainably, for example, tribes in the Amazon that have no contact with modern technology or the outside world and yet have stable populations and are healthy. The focus should be on those regions and communities that have been heavily disrupted by globalization and industrialization, communities with exploding populations and a push toward urbanization and associated migration to urban areas, lack of education, mobility, communications, basic hygiene, and nutrition.

The firm needs to create channels by which these voices can enter the firm by inviting reaction, response, or suggestions from the public at large around specific issues through face-to-face interaction, telephone access, email, or online dialogue. The corporate managers then create an inventory of potential sites and contexts where learning can take place for generating ideas for new business models that are sustainable in terms of economic potential, zero pollution or biodiversity and ecosystem disruption, and enable economic and earning capacity building in local communities. The costs of developing this capability include managerial training, time, travel, and other forms of operating slack and the benefits could include the generation of radical or disruptive ideas for products, services, and business models. Once again, the costs in terms of managerial time and effort are likely to be a fraction of what a large firm would normally spend on research and development to generate new ideas and innovations.

Reaching out and seeking knowledge from fringe stakeholders enables managers to suspend disbelief and accept information that disconfirms the existing shared mental models in the firm. Such knowledge can be generated only when managers escape from old ideas and information that confirm the existing dominant logic of the organization. Effective "fan-out" thus does not look for solutions to problems but, rather, focuses on asking the right questions of the right stakeholders to understand dynamic and complex problems that can affect future survival and competitiveness. However, the capability for fanning out to gather diverse ideas needs to be complemented with a capability to fan-in this diverse information and integrate it into the current knowledge and capabilities for sustainable innovation.

Fan-in sub-capability: Integrating diverse and disconfirming information

Once the firm's boundaries have been expanded and divergent thinking has opened up the managers of the firm both to new concerns and emerging opportunities for the future, the firm now needs to integrate this diverse information into practical, usable innovations that will be successful in the BOP context. Practical strategies emerge only after the apparent contradictions between knowledge from fringe stakeholders and the current business model have been reconciled. This often requires a reframing of a firm's dominant business logic, often by redefining the business with a focus on the consumer utility delivered rather than the firm's existing products and services (see Chapter 4).

A striking example of this reframing is GE Healthcare's shift from selling scanners costing $250,000 to upper-end hospitals in India and China to the development of an $800 Vscan machine for rural India that is portable, battery-operated, easy-to-use, and easy-to-repair.

The machine for delivering distributed onsite affordable healthcare to unserved markets was created via a process of co-creation with fringe stakeholders who were actual users in remote rural areas. The process of this innovation that used the capability of radical transactiveness is explained in more detail below.

Another example of this reframing in BOP markets is the transformation of Hindustan Unilever Ltd. (HUL), the Indian subsidiary of Unilever. For several decades, the company's products were adaptations of Unilever's internationally popular brands, successfully targeted at upper- and middle-class segments of the market. Nirma, a small upstart operation, entered the market in the early 1980s with washing products priced at a fraction of HUL's products. Within a short period, Nirma moved up-market from lower-income to middle-income markets, seriously eroding HUL's market share and profits. After struggling unsuccessfully for a decade via price competition and advertising, HUL decided to extend itself into the BOP, that is, poor rural villages that were not even targeted by Nirma. Insights gained from these radically different markets helped HUL reframe its product innovation logic from adapting international brands to developing products from the grassroots for poor consumers and moving them up-market to its traditional consumers. This strategy not only helped HUL gain back market share from Nirma but also opened up new markets and helped it meet the needs of its traditional markets better.

Diverse and disconfirming information gained from fanning out can be integrated into new practical strategies by generating complex interactions, and reconciling contradictions.

Generating complex interactions

Just as living in a different country allows managers to better identify appropriate product and service modifications in established international markets, spending time in rural areas in developing countries, especially where nature has been devastated, provides a radically different physical and mental context to spark the imagination. To be able to absorb knowledge from fringe stakeholders, however, especially those that are adversarial or peripheral to the firm's current operations, managers need to empathize with differences in perspectives. Empathy depends upon deep listening and complex interactions with those possessing divergent perspectives.

GE Healthcare's managers in India fanned out to rural health practitioners including Accredited Social Health Activists (ASHA workers) to understand the health needs of the rural poor and the challenges inherent in scanning diagnostics in remote areas. This complex interaction enabled them to understand the affordable price points for individual scans and the estimated size of the market.

HUL generates complex interactions by requiring all company employees to spend six weeks living in the BOP (India has over 630,000 rural villages) and actively seeking local consumer insights and preferences as they develop new products.[196] The company has created an R&D center in rural India that focuses specifically on technology and product development to serve the needs of the poor and sources raw materials almost exclusively from local producers. HUL uses a wide variety of local partners to distribute their products and also supports the efforts of those partners to build additional capabilities. By developing local understanding and empathy, and experimenting with co-creation of products, services, and business models, through new partnerships HUL has been able to generate substantial revenues and profits from the BOP markets. Traditionally with a focus on middle- and upper-income markets for decades, HUL now generates over half of its business in BOP markets.

In 2000, with increasing knowledge of the BOP, HUL initiated Project Shakti with a target to empower 75,000 underprivileged rural women as micro-entrepreneurs by 2015 as channels to get products directly to consumers. The Project was also intended to generate economic capacity in villages by extending HUL's reach into untapped markets and to build brands through local influencers. This business model was based on partnerships with the government-supported and microcredit-financed village self-help groups composed of women. Women were the main consumers of HUL products. Empowering women as entrepreneurs leads to greater grassroots economic development. Since most of India's 630,000 villages are remote and not connected by roads and distribution infrastructure, they offer a low business potential for larger firms and multinational enterprises. Project Shakti was a rural distribution initiative to target these small villages. The project allowed HUL to enhance its direct rural reach and also create livelihood opportunities for underprivileged rural women. The project created 45,000 women entrepreneurs in fifteen Indian states by 2013 and provides access to quality products to over 100,000 villages and over 3 million households every month.[197] This project was subsequently adapted by Unilever in several South-East Asian, African, and Latin American markets. In developing this model further, HUL also built alliances with telecommunication firms and banks to enable the Shakti entrepreneurs to sell telecom prepaid currency, sim card activations, and to act as banking correspondents. The enhanced business model doubled the income of the Shakti families and helped the community by getting better access to communication products and to banking facilities, leading to sustained prosperity.[198]

In contrast, Nike's failed attempt in the late 1990s to produce an athletic footware product for the booming low-income populations in China and other developing countries can be traced, at least in part, to a lack of complex interaction and empathy.[199] Based upon a relatively low price point ($10–15 per pair), the "World Shoe" was designed as a product that could appeal to the large numbers in the BOP who could not afford Nike's top-of-the-line products. In China, Nike relied exclusively on its existing contract factory network to produce the product, utilized the firm's established in-country channels to distribute the World Shoe, and did not develop a context-specific marketing plan for the product. In fact, the World Shoe was displayed side-by-side with the $150 Air Maxx in upscale retail outlets in Beijing and Shanghai. Relying on familiar partners and the existing business model for high-end athletic shoes resulted in the World Shoe struggling to meet its sales goals. The initiative was terminated in 2002.

Line operating managers as well as R&D and product development managers are able to generate intense interactions with fringe stakeholders only after suitable cultural and ecosystem sensitivity training. They then immerse themselves in radically different contexts to transfer tacit knowledge about the needs of consumers that they do not cater to with existing products. As a result, they come to understand the potential for, and feasibility of, applying innovative technologies to develop new business models and products. For example, Procter & Gamble has launched a pilot venture in rural Nicaragua to help its managers generate creative ideas by immersing themselves in a context where the company currently has no presence, infrastructure or partners. By doing so, they avoid having the voices from the fringe contaminated by the dominant logic of the marketing model used to serve their existing markets. As the HUL and P&G experiences demonstrate, the costs in managerial time and travel for generating complex interactions are a fraction of what a large firm spends on marketing research and product development for established markets. Regardless of costs, such immersion is essential in order to compete for a sustainable future. To illustrate, an American coal-based electric utility will find it hard to imagine future growth trajectories, disruptive innovations, and radical business models in distributed solar power generation without immersing itself in a context where centralized gigantic grids of fossil fuel based power generation do not exist.

Reconciling contradictions

Generating complex interactions with fringe stakeholders at the BOP yields information that may disconfirm, conflict with, or contradict current mental models of the firm's managers. GE Healthcare had to reconcile contradictions between the model of very high margins on a small number of scanners to a few upper-end hospitals and selling large quantities of very low-margin portable hand-held cheap Vscans that would make them available in every village. HUL had to reconcile contradictions between a centralized distribution model and establishing thousands of grassroots entrepreneurs who were consumers as well as sellers of their products in small quantities. On the other hand, Nike was unable to reconcile the apparent disconnect between its current business model and the needs and requirements of the new, low-income BOP consumer it was trying to serve. In fact, designing and producing a lower-cost shoe using the existing business mindset, models, and systems meant, paradoxically, that Nike failed to reach its target BOP customer. Thus, integrating diverse and disconfirming information into strategy requires reconciliation of seemingly conflicting perspectives. Competitive imagination is sparked only when the organization commits to resolving the contradictions created by the disconfirming information introduced by fringe stakeholders.

Mexico's largest cement company, Cemex, was able to develop a very profitable BOP strategy in Mexico and other developing markets such as Bangladesh, Egypt, Indonesia, Thailand, Colombia, Costa Rica, Nicaragua, and the Dominican Republic.[200] The poor in these markets are not only unserved or under-served, but sales to the poor tend to be less subject to volatility based upon macroeconomic conditions. Cemex embarked on a strategy of learning how to tap the enormous BOP market in developing countries by first studying how to do business with the poor in Mexico. Poor, do-it-yourself homebuilders in urban slums and shantytowns often take four years to complete just one room and thirteen years to finish a small four-room house. This is because banks and other businesses will not engage with poor residents of informal settlements where legal status of their property ownership is murky. Haphazard design combined with material theft and spoilage conspire to make home construction for the poor a costly and risky proposition.

To reach this market, Cemex had to reconcile these contradictions by creating a new business model. Through its program called "Patrimonio Hoy" set up in 1998, Cemex formed savings clubs that allow aspiring homebuilders to make weekly savings payments. In exchange, Cemex provides material storage and architectural support so that homes can be well designed and built in sensible stages. Patrimonio Hoy provides these products at average market prices and also provides micro-financing (over $135 million advanced to date), technical advice, and logistical support to assist participants in building their own homes. The program has established a collaborative network of distributors that are mainly women trained and empowered through the program to build trust and secure participation of community members and the families themselves. In addition to housing, Patrimonio Hoy also helps improve the local public school infrastructure, including classrooms, bathrooms, and sports facilities, with the active participation of the program participants. The result is that participants in the program build their houses three times faster, of higher quality, and at a third the cost to build an average home in Mexico. Patrimonio Hoy has been growing 250 percent per year, has enrolled more than 35,000 poor families since its inception, and has provided affordable housing solutions to almost one million people. The market value of homes built through Patrimonio Hoy is approximately 20 percent higher than comparable homes due to the higher quality and functionality of the structures.[201] In reducing the environmental footprint of the program, it is introducing energy-efficient appliances to help participants reduce energy usage and costs.

Reconciling contradictions involves incubating disruptive innovations in a transactive mode with fringe stakeholders. At this stage, radical new ideas and business models identified in the previous steps are operationalized and implemented. Such implementation takes into account the concerns of remote stakeholders affected by the firm's operations to anticipate needs and prevent the creation of adversarial swarms of stakeholders. At early stages, it is useful to create a corporate-level clearinghouse for radical new business models in order to provide initial resources and gain the blessing of top management. In this way, efforts of individual project teams can be better coordinated and experience more effectively diffused. For example, Unilever has created an international committee to transfer and adapt innovations such as HUL's products and promotion programs to other countries and markets. In recognition of the disruptive innovations that have emerged from HUL and other grassroots initiatives, Unilever has begun adding managers from these developing country subsidiaries to its board of directors and top management committees at the head office. Such diversity is now paying dividends in the form of increased innovation in conventional R&D and product development.

The sub-capability requires the development of processes and routines including:

- Coordination and exchange of information in organizational committees that are horizontally (strategic business units, functional areas, geographic locations) and vertically (cut across corporate hierarchies) diverse

- Incubation of new innovations and business models by setting up taskforces consisting of operating managers, R&D engineers and staff managers, some of whom have experienced the radically different stakeholder contexts

- Ongoing transactiveness with stakeholders in radical contexts to test and refine ideas for products, services, and business models to ensure that stakeholder needs are met and their concerns regarding negative social and environmental impacts taken care of

- Organizing facilitated stakeholder dialogues involving line managers, product developers, and technologists in collaboration with fringe stakeholder representatives to develop a specific new product concept, market, or situation

- Exploring the feasibility of innovations in current business contexts and transfer to other businesses, markets, and business units

The costs of this sub-capability are the investments in manpower and processes for the coordination, ongoing transactiveness, and engagement with stakeholders. The benefits are the generation of disruptive innovations in products, services, and business models while addressing the economic, social, and environmental concerns of stakeholders at the fringe and preventing the creation of adversarial swarms.

The integration of diverse and disconfirming information is a creative process involving the design of new products and business models to serve previously invisible needs. This step focuses on the articulation and implementation of practical solutions to the problems and opportunities identified in the "fan-out" stage. The challenge is thus to link both stages of the RT approach together into a coherent process for new strategy formulation and implementation. Together, the capabilities of stakeholder "fan-out" and "fan-in" reinforce each other. By integrating knowledge from fringe stakeholders, radical transactiveness has the potential to challenge fundamental business models and frames of reference, leading to new bases of competitive advantage, initially in the BOP and then in middle-income and high-income markets, as the example of GE's portable ECG machine described below shows.

Examples: GE's portable ECG machine and Godrej & Boyce's Chotukool

GE Healthcare is a market leader in the manufacture of ECG machines and scanners used for medical imaging. These machines are expensive and range from $250,000 to $500,000. Therefore, a scan using these machines costs between about $20 and $500. Moreover, the machines are complex, heavy, bulky, and require a skilled technician to operate them. They also require skilled technicians for elaborate service support. These factors made the machines irrelevant for the BOP in a major market for GE, rural India. Patients could not afford the high price of a scan and the small clinics and physicians couldn't afford the expensive machines and the service and support (electricity) costs.

As its BOP Healthy-imagination strategy, GE Healthcare set itself a challenge to develop an $800 scanner machine for rural India that was portable, battery-operated, easy-to-use, and easy-to-repair. GE found many ways to cut costs. The high-end machine was custom-designed, so GE Healthcare's Indian managers fanned out to engage rural health practitioners and fanned-in with the learning generated to co-create a machine using commonly available standard components, realizing huge cost advantages. For a cost-effective printer, GE used the kind of ticket printer found on public buses and in movie theaters. Since these printers are produced in the millions, GE could enjoy significantly lower costs due to economies of scale. The small printer reduced the weight of the machine to less than a can of soda and helped make it portable. By eliminating the monitor, GE reduced the need for huge power consumption. This, in turn, contributed to longer life for the rechargeable battery. The machine is easy to operate and use by people who cannot read or write and cannot follow detailed instructions. A "green" button indicates start and a "red" button means stop. GE did away with the need for extensive service support, designing the machine with a few standard modules that can be easily replaced. If the device failed, users could swap modules. GE's innovation in India has transformed its global business, since the machine is sold in more than 90 countries. This is an example of a BOP-generated product that has been scaled up to developed markets.[202]

Godrej & Boyce, an Indian company, produces home products and appliances including refrigerators. In an effort to crack the BOP market, initially the firm manufactured a smaller and cheaper version of its middle-income refrigerator. However, this product failed in the BOP market. The company's managers decided to fan-out and spend time in the field embedding themselves and engaging in deep dialogue with members of rural households and rural shops. They concluded that these homes did not need cheaper and smaller refrigerators. The BOP consumers needed an affordable way to preserve milk, dairy products, vegetables, and leftovers for a day or two and prevent them from spoiling. According to the United Nations Commission on Sustainable Development, due to the unaffordability and lack of preservation and storage, one-third of all food in India is lost to spoilage.

Godrej developed several prototypes to seek feedback at "co-creation" events with consumers in the BOP. The product that the BOP consumers liked was ChotuKool, or "little cool" in Hindi. Instead of traditional compressors, ChotuKool is based on a thermoelectric chip that maintains a cool temperature on a 12-volt DC current or on an external battery that can be charged using solar energy. Its unconventional design ensures that cold air settles down in the cabinet to minimize heat loss and power consumption. The unit is easily portable, with 45 liters of volume inside a fully plastic body weighing less than 10 pounds. Priced at $69, about half the price of an entry-level refrigerator, Chotukool created a new product category, opening up a market of billions at the BOP.

While the capability of radical transactiveness enables the firm to identify the fringe stakeholders that could potentially help build competitive imagination of future sustainable innovations, undertake deep listening, generate complex interactions to foster higher-order learning, and reconcile contradictions between the firm's existing mental models and external information, strategic bridging is a useful strategy to overcome barriers to successful implementation of sustainable business models at the BOP.

Strategic bridging

Developing BOP contexts are radically different from the developed market and upper- to middle-income contexts that most large corporations and multinational enterprises are used to operating in. BOP contexts are often characterized by tribal societies within which communities and individuals owe greater (or their only) loyalty to tribal hierarchies rather than to their state and federal governments. This is especially true in Africa where many countries' boundaries have been drawn by colonial powers, splitting an ethnic tribe into two or sometimes three or four countries.[203] In such contexts, firms may face institutional environments characterized by high levels of corruption. Traditional alliances with governments and state-owned institutions often require strategies and business models that may not be consistent with the firm's values of ethical conduct and may lead to less than optimal and sustainable outcomes. In fact, a direct approach to the government or a state-owned institution in such contexts is often rejected outright if it is perceived that a partnership with the firm will not enable the political and bureaucratic officials to further their personal agendas. Therefore, a process of radical transactiveness involving fringe stakeholders at the grassroots has the greatest potential for long-term success because it involves large numbers of individuals who are the foundation or the base of the economy and society. The power of the stakeholders and communities at the grassroots to achieve political and institutional change toward a sustainable society is much greater than the power of the individual firm.

In such contexts, it is critical for the firm to embed itself at the grassroots in order to understand the social and cultural backgrounds and motivations of the local (and fringe) stakeholders in order to develop a successful sustainable business model. In traditional strategic alliances the focus is on the resolution of differences in the economic agenda of the various parties. In the BOP context, this is complicated by the need to develop a model that will address not only the economic agendas but also the cultural, social, political, and environmental agendas of the stakeholders. Therefore, the firm has the additional responsibility of helping the various stakeholders crystallize the problem domain in terms of the critical and common economic, social, and environmental issues facing the constituents. It then has an opportunity to co-create a sustainable business model that offers solutions for the various agendas of the stakeholders involved. A business model that addresses the main problem issue facing each constituent organization or group will enable them to obtain commitment from their respective members, other constituents with similar agendas, and especially the fringe constituents.[204]

An approach that has been successfully adopted is one where the firm acts as a strategic bridge between organizations that cannot collaborate directly due to widely different missions, or for political, institutional, or bureaucratic reasons. The concept of strategic bridging is a distinct form of collaboration where a firm spans the gap among diverse constituencies to find joint solutions to a complex problem domain.[205] Strategic bridging is particularly useful in sustainable development, due to the inability of any one organization to span the entire problem domain covering the several economic, social, cultural, and ecological issues involved. In strategic bridging, the firm links diverse island organizations that are distinct in terms of resources, personnel, and missions while enabling the achievement of the goals of all the organizations. Bridges do not result in the creation of an independent third-party organization with an independent mission, as in the case of joint ventures or multiparty task forces. Unlike mediators, bridges enter collaborative negotiations to further their own ends as well as to serve as links among domain stakeholders. An important difference between strategic bridging and other forms of collaboration is the need for the bridge to obtain back-home commitment from its constituents-because it remains at all times an independent entity with its own agenda.

Strategic bridging is a potential implementation solution to development problems where the other parties to the collaboration are unable to negotiate directly due to mistrust, tradition, logistical problems, or there is need for an impartial external third party to restore a balance of power, resources, and expertise between the prospective collaborators. Strategic bridging is most effective when the problem domain is ill defined and the need exists for problem crystallization via the involvement of the bridge.[206]

Multinational enterprises have sometimes been able to build a sustainable business model at the BOP by acting as a bridge between an international infrastructure lender and the state government. In one case described by Sharma, Vredenberg and Westley,[207] an international lending organization could not lend infrastructure development funds directly to the federal and state governments due to past defaults and gross mismanagement of funds. However, the lender was able to work through a multinational enterprise that acted as a bridge to develop a business model that incorporated the implementation of the infrastructure project as a part of its own business model while simultaneously generating environmental benefits and social benefits for the local community and tribes.[208] Another organization that has operated as a strategic bridge is Care Enterprise Partners (CEP), a subsidiary of Care Canada. CEP was formed with a mission to stitch together sustainable business models between multinationals such as DuPont, HUL, the Tata Group, ITC (the Indian subsidiary of BAT plc), and local stakeholders including NGOs, local communities, and local governments. Several of my students worked with CEP in India to help design these business models. Some of these business models were successful and have been scaled up; many were ultimately unsuccessful but generated a great deal of learning for all partners including the multinationals and Care Canada.

Strategic bridging makes collaborations possible where the island organizations are unable to negotiate directly due to past mistrust or other traditional, procedural, social, cultural, and political problems. At the same time, the independence of mission of the collaborating organizations is not compromised. For example, due to their missions, environmental NGOs are often unable to enter into a direct alliance with a for-profit business but they can achieve their goals of effecting change in business via a bridging organization.

Summary

Competing at the base of the pyramid offers a potential for tremendous rewards for firms due to the immense size of the market and the potential for disruptive innovation that can be scaled up into business models in developing and developed markets. At the same time, this market is very different from the high-income and middle-income markets with which firms are familiar. During the past decade, hundreds of firms have attempted to sell scaled-down, cheaper products in these markets and have either failed, or succeeded without generating positive social and environmental impacts. Competing in the BOP is not about exploiting the poor to generate profits but about improving their lives by meeting unmet fundamental needs of hygiene, health, education, communication, access to markets, energy, shelter, and nutrition. Due to the foreignness of BOP markets, the most viable approach is co-creation through engagement of, and embedded deep dialogue with, the consumers and the value chain in the BOP.

Firms that have developed the mega-capability of radical transactiveness (RT) have been relatively more successful in co-creating successful business models for the BOP with positive economic, social, and environmental benefits. This mega-capability of RT leverages and capitalizes upon the critical capabilities discussed in Chapter 6. This capability requires firms to develop a set of sub-capabilities or processes to "fan-out" to identify fringe stakeholders by following the linkages of existing stakeholder networks to the periphery; and to go beyond the traditional logic of stakeholder salience to consciously seek out remote stakeholders that are non-legitimate, non-urgent, and powerless. Networking from the core to the periphery helps to identify emergent stakeholder concerns in order to prevent the formation of adversarial swarms. Putting the last first reverses the logic of the established business and seeks to generate imagination and ideas about unmet needs, potential new products, and sustainable business innovations.

The process of fanning-in requires building the managerial sub-capability or capacity for empathizing with diverse and disconfirming BOP stakeholder perspectives, understanding the culture, thought processes, and language of distant stakeholders, and acquiring the sub-capability to reconcile the contradictions between the existing business model and the views of fringe BOP stakeholders. By generating complex interactions, it is possible to develop the intimacy and trust needed for honest two-way exchanges to occur between managers and those on the fringe of the company's established stakeholder network. To convert this insight into practical business strategies, however, it is crucial to reconcile the contradictions between the current reality and the needs and requirements of the BOP context.

However, developing a business model is only a part of the process to ensure success in the BOP. Implementation of these business models successfully requires the involvement of multiple constituents who have different agendas and missions. Therefore, the firm plays a role in crystallizing the problem domain to reflect the complexity of the economic, social, environmental, and political issues that are important to various constituents. It then ensures that the business model it develops addresses the domain or overlap issues. Moreover, sometimes some constituents operating in the BOP are unable to directly collaborate with each other due to past mistrust or divergent goals and missions or ideologies. The firm can create a business model to stitch the various constituencies together by playing the role of a strategic bridge via which the various constituents can collaborate and achieve their goals while enabling the firm to draw upon the resources and capabilities of these constituents to implement a successful sustainable business model at the BOP.

Eight
No business is an island

Our most basic common link is that we all inhabit this planet. We all breathe the same air. We all cherish our children's future. And we are all mortal.

John F. Kennedy

Sustainability is a journey and not a destination. No organization, whether it is a business or an NGO or a government agency, can hope to become completely sustainable in terms of having perfectly positive social and environmental footprints and achieving its core objectives. In fact, some non-business organizations such as the armed forces have historically had very large negative environmental impacts (such as the use and disposal of toxic chemicals) and social impacts (such as civilian deaths and the displacement of large numbers of people from their homes). Perhaps a firm's quest for a sustainable business is as utopian as the quest for a sustainable world on the part of some members of society. However, that should certainly not be a rationale for not undertaking this quest or for avoiding action. As this book argues, the quest for a sustainable world is an opportunity and a catalyst for business to innovate and build not only the products, services, and business models of tomorrow but also the organizational forms of tomorrow. The late Ray Anderson, ex-CEO of Interface, used to call this quest the "sustainability mountain." With each environmental and social action and practice adopted, with each new measurement and goal achieved, managers in the company are able to visualize and realize the magnitude of the challenges that lie ahead and the tremendous changes that need to be made in order to compete in this world that faces tremendous sustainability challenges. The ongoing global debates during the past two decades make it clear that, regardless of differences of opinion and skepticism, the world's institutions and businesses have been progressing toward, rather than away from, social and environmental sustainability.

The previous chapters in this book describe the building blocks for a firm that sets out on this journey: the steps it needs to take in order to identify salient sustainability issues, link sustainable practices to competitive advantage, build logic for a core sustainable business proposition, build motivations, and build capacity for a sustainable organization that is ready to compete for the future. This involves strategically analyzing its sustainability footprint in the context of its salient stakeholder networks, mapping the risks of an unsustainable strategy, understanding the competitive benefits of generating sustainable value (positive economic, social, and environmental impacts), developing business logic in terms of core value proposition and customer utility to guide the firm's evolution toward sustainability, changing managerial mind-sets by creating an opportunity frame that enables them to view the sustainability challenges as opportunities, building critical capabilities for stakeholder integration, organizational learning and continuous innovation, and developing future business growth opportunities in emerging markets at the base of the pyramid where the challenges of developing sustainable business models are significantly different, and social and environmental challenges are enmeshed and require a mega-capability of radical transactiveness.

It is clear that a firm must first develop the motivation to act (strategic analysis of its sustainability footprint, understanding the risks and benefits of a sustainability strategy, developing a sustainable business logic and an opportunity frame for managerial decision-making) in order to effectively develop and deploy its capacity (capabilities) to compete in a world that is journeying toward a sustainable future. While it is inevitable that a firm may acquire some technical capabilities via mergers or collaborations, it needs to build the critical capabilities for sustainable innovation (Chapter 6) in-house. If a firm seeks only to acquire the critical capabilities for a sustainable capacity externally, it will be unlikely to generate sustainable innovations without an organizational context within which its managers participate in the journey and the learning process. It is difficult to acquire capabilities externally and have sustainable business logic baked into managerial DNA and motivate them to seek opportunities for a sustainable future.

At the same time, as societal understanding of social and environmental challenges and the meaning of sustainability continue to evolve, the firm has to become an active partner in this evolution instead of trying to constantly catch up. Therefore, firms need to embed within their organization a continuous process of analyzing its sustainability footprint, understanding evolving stakeholder networks, quantifying emerging risks and benefits, building managerial motivations to acts, investing in critical capabilities, and engaging BOP markets via radical transactiveness.

However, even with the best of motivations and capacity, it is virtually impossible for a firm to become sustainable on its own. The Kalundborg model discussed in Chapter 3 describes collaboration between industries, agriculture, and public utilities. The symbiotic complexity of the Kalundborg model has not been replicated thus far. However, that is an excellent example of how regional groupings of for-profit firms, public utilities, local governments, farmers, and communities can create more sustainable regional systems, whether by eliminating waste or creating an equitable society. Similarly, Chapter 7 makes it clear that successful BOP models that have the widest range of positive economic, social, and environmental impacts involve collaborations and co-creation among businesses, local communities, NGOs, and local governments. When it comes to achieving sustainability, no firm is an island. For that matter, nor is a town, city, community, local or federal government, or an NGO. In collaboration with multiple partners, it may be possible for an individual entity to make rapid progress toward more sustainable operations. In Chapters t2, 6, and 7, this book discusses how firms can engage diverse stakeholders to develop an in-depth understanding of the interface of its business with society and the natural environment and gather information to catalyze learning for sustainable innovation. In Chapter 6, this book discusses how firms can build collaborations with NGOs, governments, and universities to build and acquire capabilities. Moreover, academic institutions such as universities have become valuable partners with business and industry associations to unravel the science of social and environmental interfaces of business and help develop solutions. This chapter discusses the critical role of the political environment, consumers, and the value chain of business in this journey.

The political environment

The political environment of business in its home country and the countries it operates in plays a most important role in facilitating or hindering a firm's journey toward sustainability. The political environment may range from mostly free market, such as the US, to a highly regulated centralized economy such as China. Even in relatively free markets, the government may choose to regulate some aspects of social and environmental impacts and not others. For example, at a federal or state level, the levying of a carbon tax enables firms to achieve competitive advantage if they have a proactive sustainability strategy to reduce or eliminate their carbon emissions. In such contexts, firms that emit large quantities of CO_2 struggle to compete and lobby governments to reverse policies. However, polluting firms may succeed in lobbying against regulations in such economies.

The most recent example characterized by political twists and turns is the levying of a carbon tax in Australia in 2012. Initially, the liberal Australian government had to make some initial concessions to mining and resource extraction companies so that they could maintain their global competitive advantage for a few years. Initial credits were issued to three of the biggest polluters: Alcoa of Australia Ltd. (the mining/refining subsidiary of the American Aluminum Company), and two to Queensland Nitrates Pty Ltd. for production of ammonia and ammonia nitrate. The three were given a total of 6.37 million free carbon credits as an "assistance program" to companies that "produce significant carbon emissions but are constrained in their ability to pass through costs in global markets."[209] The election of the conservative government under prime minister Tony Abbott in 2013 is changing the landscape in the reverse direction and against the proactive companies since the new government has pledged to eliminate the carbon tax. While this is a backward step, it does encourage several companies to avoid developing a sustainable strategy.

Several European countries have been leaders in creating and sustaining carbon markets via cap-and-trade policies in the European Union. The global recession and subsequent drop in industrial activity led to a drop in the price of carbon from $40 per ton in August 2008 to around $4 per ton in 2013. This has led to a lower competitiveness of renewable energy and a drop in investments in solar and wind ventures in Europe and across the world.[210] It is hoped that an acceleration of economic activity in Europe will once again revive the carbon markets and investments in renewable energy. At the same time, badly designed subsidies in some European countries favor the burning of wood for fuel.

While some carbon initiatives are languishing, others are emerging. In 2012 California launched AB32, the official name of the state's carbon cap-and-trade system. AB32 commits California to reduce its greenhouse gas emissions to 1990 levels by 2020, a 17 percent cut. The reduction is set to be achieved by putting a cap on the state's carbon emissions that is gradually tightened by about 2 to 3 percent per year. Companies covered under the law need to either reduce their carbon emissions to meet the tightening cap or purchase carbon allowances on a regulated market to compensate for their emissions.[211] Thus, even though regulations may work imperfectly for the first few years, they are critical for creating a level playing field to create incentives for innovation.

The US Climate Action Partnership, a collaboration of leading businesses and environmental groups, has called on the US federal government several times since the mid 2000s to enact legislation to regulate and reduce greenhouse gas emissions. The Partnership includes the CEOs of Duke Energy, DuPont, Dow Chemical, and GE among other companies, and has testified before the US Congress, arguing that the inability of the US government to articulate a clear policy on climate change is eroding US competitiveness while firms in countries with stringent climate change policies are building capabilities and technologies for the future with support from their governments. The lack of a US policy means that US companies would be at a competitive disadvantage even in their own very large market at home if they invested in clean technologies, renewable energy, and climate change solutions without government support.[212] Even in the future, if and when the US government was to finally formulate a policy, some global companies in Europe and Australia may have a major head start because they have been forced to develop the capabilities for sustainable innovation and have begun to develop innovative technologies and business models. Similarly, the changes in the political environment in Australia and changes in regulations have not caused the most proactive Australian companies to change course, but rather have created disincentives for the reactive companies to adopt a more sustainable strategy.

Proactive firms with a sustainability agenda need not be passive recipients of changes in the political and regulatory environment. They can lobby for pro-sustainability legislation including the removal of subsidies that encourage the waste of resources and generation of toxic pollution; they can advocate for market-based environmental policies; and they can become leaders in helping develop full-cost (incorporating the social and environmental costs of a firm's operations) accounting standards.[213] Building a sustainable organization is a patient long-term evolution and short-term fluctuations in policy do not deter companies that believe that within a sustainable future for the world lie competitive opportunities for business. Moreover, the BOP is a context where it is possible to engage local communities and local governments in integrated sustainable business models.

Consumers and communities

Consumers play an increasing role in the transformation of business. A great deal of positive change in business has happened as a result of pressure from civil society (communities and NGOs) and consumers. However, there are billions of consumers globally who are not aware or educated about the negative social and environmental impacts of business. At the same time, there are billions who are either in survival mode at the BOP or aspire to consume the basic comforts of life before they can exercise a social or environmental conscience. It is frightening to think of the tremendous strain on the environment and resources as the aspirations of these billions are met. Yet, one cannot deny them the standard of living and the quality of life that the rich have enjoyed for several centuries. Hence, it is urgent and critical that business engages consumers and communities in the BOP to develop sustainable business models that help restore the environment and social equity rather than exacerbating the negative effects of rapid industrialization.

It is easy for business to blame consumers for their lack of action and it is easy for consumers to blame business for continuing to bombard them with frivolous products and services that are unsustainable. If a business has to compete in a sustainable world, consumers have to become partners and co-creators not only in the BOP but also in developed markets. Firms with a sustainability agenda play a role in consumer literacy, often starting with education programs in schools where students are the most open to such ideas. Such firms also align the sustainability values of their managers with the values of the external constituents in their stakeholder networks, and thereby catalyze socio-cultural change at the grassroots.[214] While this may sound idealistic, such socio-cultural change is in the interest of companies developing the sustainable products, services, and business models of tomorrow. For example, when DuPont developed substitutes for ozone-depleting CFCs (of which it was the largest global manufacturer), it played the role of a catalyst in bringing together governments, NGOs, and major companies to establish the Montreal Protocol to eliminate CFCs in 1987.

The value chain

Even with enlightened government policies and regulations, no firm is an island in developing and implementing a strategy to create sustainable value. As discussed in Chapter 6, the development of critical capabilities requires collaboration and partnerships with multiple stakeholders. As the Kalundborg example described in Chapter 3 shows, it is extremely difficult for an individual facility or a firm to achieve zero emissions and wastes on its own. However, it can work toward this objective by working with other firms, with suppliers, with distributors, with communities, with governments, and with NGOs. A firm's value chain is complex and global and understanding the impacts along the value chain requires partnering with suppliers and customers, a process that Wal-Mart has begun.

If firms are serious about building a competitive imagination about products, services, and business models that will enable them to compete in a sustainable world, they have to make investment decisions with a consideration of not only how they will reduce and prevent wastes but also where they can locate or who they can partner with to create closed-loop waste exchange systems and greater social benefits. They will have to make decisions based on the costs of paying fair living wages and providing attractive working conditions rather than finding the cheapest contractors in the lowest wage markets. They will have to develop business models based on fair prices to farmers, craftsmen, and small suppliers. They will have to continuously invest in pilot projects (in collaboration with other stakeholders) that require patient capital but have the potential to yield breakthrough technologies, processes, and systems that can address sustainability challenges while generating shareholder value in the long term. All this while, they should be prepared to exercise leadership to influence governments to enact public policy and regulations that will support and foster sustainable businesses.

If indeed an increasing number of successful cross-sector collaborations between business, government, civil society, communities, and citizens develop in the coming years, can we halt further deterioration to the planet and to threatened species and marginalized societies, and begin to repair and reverse some of the negative impacts that have accelerated since the Industrial Revolution? It is hard to make a positive prediction with confidence, given past history of failed cross-sector collaborations around the shared objective of a sustainable world and given the skepticism that still surrounds the irrefutable science of climate change. However, firms acting in their self-interest have the potential to generate the positive impacts that international agreements and regimes have failed to achieve, such as the lead taken by DuPont in banning CFCs, albeit purely in its own self-interest. Business can take the lead to transform a substantial portion of the global economy as a force of positive social and environmental impact. If businesses are able to innovate products, services, and business models that are not only sustainable but attractive for consumers and deliver utility better, faster, and more cheaply, consumers will rapidly come on board. Consumers are at the heart of a free market society and have the power to elect politicians who will enact legislation to support sustainable business. The transformation of the political landscape will rapidly bring large numbers of reactive businesses on board. However, if business cannot play such a transformative role, a substantial sector of business and society will continue to support unsustainable policies and legislation, accelerating the sustainability challenges the world faces. A great deal of discussion about sustainability centers on the negative impact of human (and specifically industrial) activity on our planet Earth. The billions of years of history of the Earth tell us that in the long term, our planet is resilient and will take corrective action. It is humanity and its activities (including business) that will be destroyed rather than the Earth. Let us act upon one of the greatest opportunities of our time and foster business as the power for good economically, socially, and ecologically.

Endnotes

Chapter 1

1 WCED, *Our Common Future* (New York: Oxford University Press, 1987).

Chapter 2

2 Personal conversation with Ray Anderson in Atlanta, December 2009.

3 www.walmartstores.com/Sustainability/9292.aspx (accessed May 15, 2012).

4 www.pg.com/en_US/sustainability/environmental_sustainability/products_packaging/index.shtml (accessed May 15, 2012).

5 This discussion draws upon the concepts in R.K. Mitchell, B.R. Agle and D.J. Wood, "Toward a Theory of Stakeholder Identification and Salience: Defining the Principle of Who and What Really Counts," *Academy of Management Review* 22(4) (1997): 853-86.

6 J. Frooman, "Stakeholder Influence Strategies," *Academy of Management Review* 24(2) (1999): 191-205.

7 *Ibid.*

8 This discussion is based on the following study in the Canadian forest products industry: S. Sharma and I. Henriques, "Stakeholder Influences on Sustainability Practices in the Canadian Forest Products Industry," *Strategic Management Journal* 26(2) (2005): 159-80.

9 http://en.wikipedia.org/wiki/Keystone_Pipeline (accessed October 27, 2013).

10 S. Greenhouse, "Retailers Split on Contrition after Bangladesh Factory Collapse," *The New York Times* online edition (April 30, 2013).

11 E. Simanis and S. Hart, *The Monsanto Company: Quest for Sustainability* (Washington, DC: World Resources Institute, 2000).

12 http://occupywallstreet.net/ (accessed August 11, 2013).

13 *Ibid.*

14 "Nightline Tours Apple Supplier Foxconn: Get an Unprecedented Look at the Factory," *The Huffington Post* (February 22, 2012).

15 "When the Jobs Inspector Calls," *The Economist* (March 31, 2012): 73-6.

16 *Ibid.*

17 Greenhouse, "Retailers Split on Contrition."

18 S.M. Llana and I.Evans, "In Bangladesh Factory Aftermath, US and European Firms Take Different Paths," *The Christian Science Monitor* online edition (May 29, 2013).

19 For an empirical examination of how indirect or secondary stakeholders affect a firm's practices, see Sharma and Henriques, "Stakeholder Influences on Sustainability Practices in the Canadian Forest Products Industry."

20 "Supermäjordammerung," *The Economist* (August 3 to 9, 2013): 20-22.

21 www.arb.ca.gov/cc/capandtrade/capandtrade.htm (accessed August 11, 2013). "California's Cap-and-Trade Program took effect in early 2012. The enforceable compliance obligation begins on January 1, 2013, for greenhouse gas (GHG) emissions."

22 www.sasb.org (accessed July 31, 2013). The Sustainability Accounting Standards Board is a nonprofit organization that provides standards for use by publicly-listed corporations in the US in disclosing material sustainability issues. SASB standards are designed for disclosure in mandatory filings to the Securities and Exchange Commission (SEC), such as the Form 10-K and 20-F.

23 www.footprintnetwork.org/en (accessed May 5, 2013).

24 www.equator-principles.com/ (accessed May 15, 2012).

25 http://en.wikipedia.org/wiki/Radioactive_decay (accessed August 11, 2013).

26 www.epa.gov/tri/tridata/index.html (accessed October 31, 2012).

27 www.ec.gc.ca/inrp-npri/default.asp?lang=En&n=B85A1846-1 (accessed October 31, 2012).

28 www.walmartstores.com/Sustainability/9292.aspx (accessed May 15, 2012).

29 WWF, "Mangrove Forests Protected Areas from 2004 Tsunami Says New Study," November 18, 2005. http://news.mongabay.com/2005/1118-wwf.html (accessed May 15, 2012).

30 "Dash for cash," *The Economist* (August 24, 2013): 13-14.

31 http://en.wikipedia.org/wiki/Nike_sweatshops (accessed May 15, 2012).

32 A detailed description is provided in the case Brent Spar (A) & (B). IMD/Babson College. European case Clearing House.

33 S.L. Hart and S. Sharma, "Engaging Fringe Stakeholders for Competitive Imagination," *Academy of Management Executive* 18(1) (2004): 7-18.

34 C.K. Prahalad and S. Hart, "The Fortune at the Bottom of the Pyramid," *Strategy+Business* 26 (2002): 54-67.

35 *Ibid.*

36 J. McGregor, "GE: Reinventing Tech for the Emerging World," *Bloomberg Businessweek* (April 16, 2008).

Chapter 3

37 Michael E. Porter, *Competitive Advantage: Creating and Sustaining Superior Performance* (New York: Free Press, 1985).

38 P. Lacy, T. Cooper, R. Hayward and L. Neuberger, *A New Era of Sustainability: CEO reflections on progress to date, challenges ahead and the impact of the journey toward a sustainable economy* (Accenture–UN Global Compact, 2010).

39 http://en.wikipedia.org/wiki/Non-governmental_organization (accessed October 30, 2013).

40 http://en.wikipedia.org/wiki/Bhopal_disaster (accessed May 15, 2012).

41 http://en.wikipedia.org/wiki/Exxon_Valdez_oil_spill (accessed May 15, 2012).

42 http://en.wikipedia.org/wiki/Deepwater_Horizon (accessed January 1, 2013).

43 www.epa.gov/superfund/ (accessed July 23, 2012).

44 http://en.wikipedia.org/wiki/Deepwater_Horizon_oil_spill (accessed May 15, 2012).

45 *Ibid.*

46 Brent Spar (A) & (B). IMD/Babson College. European case Clearing House.

47 "Dash for Cash", *The Economist* (August 24, 2013): 13-14.

48 S. Sharma and H. Vredenburg, "Proactive Environmental Responsiveness Strategy and the Development of Competitively Valuable Organizational Capabilities," *Strategic Management Journal* 19(8) (1998): 729-53; S.L. Hart and G. Ahuja, "Does it Pay to be Green?" *Business Strategy and the Environment* 5 (1996): 30-7.

49   http://solutions.3m.com/wps/portal/3M/en_US/3M-Sustainability/Global/ Environment/3P/ (accessed June 5, 2012).

50   Dow's Sustainability Journey, www.dow.com/sustainability/ (accessed June 5, 2012).The program is also described in detail at Kenneth Baker, *Dow Chemical Company (A): The WRAP Program* (Washington, DC: World Resources Institute, 1994).

51   www2.dupont.com/Sustainability/en_US/ (accessed June 5, 2012).

52   www.intel.com/about/corporateresponsibility/environment/operations.htm (accessed June 5, 2012).

53   Personal conversation with Janet Bombardier, Senior Location Executive, IBM Essex Vermont.

54   "IBM Vermont facility receives Most Valuable Pollution Prevention award,". *Vermont Business Magazine* (October 24, 2013), http://vermon tbiz.com/news/october/ibm-vermont-facility-receives-most-valuable- pollution-prevention-award?utm_source=VBM+Mailing+List&utm_ campaign=d558495413-Enews_10_24_201310_24_2013&utm_medium= email&utm_term=0_85838110bc-d558495413-286289682 (accessed November 1, 2013).

55   Presentation by Paul Tebo at the Sustainable Enterprise Academy, 2003, Vancouver.

56   T.P. Morgan, "IBM to Recycle Silicon Wafers for Solar Cells," *IT Jungle* (November 5, 2007), www.itjungle.com/tfh/tfh110507-story05.html (accessed July 23, 2012).

57   A.B. Lovins, L.H. Lovins and P. Hawken, "A Road Map for Natural Capitalism," *Harvard Business Review* 77(3) (May-June 1999): 145-59.

58   M. Ramsay, "Ford Plans New F-150 with Aluminum Body," *The Wall Street Journal* online US edition (July 27, 2012) (accessed September 4, 2013).

59   R. Herman, S.A. Ardekani and J.H. Ausubel, "Dematerialization," in J.H. Ausubel and H.E. Sladovich (eds.), *Technology and Environment* (Washington, DC: National Academy Press, 1989): 50-69.

60   S. Shankland, "Breakthrough Material is Barely More Than Air," *Cnet* (November 18, 2011), http://news.cnet.com/8301-30685_3-57327382- 264/breakthrough-material-is-barely-more-than-air/ (accessed September 10, 2013).

61   S. Rothenberg, "Sustainability Through Servicizing," *MIT Sloan Management Review* 48(2) (2007): 83-91.

62   *Ibid.*

63   R.R. Westerman, *Tires: Reducing solid wastes and manufacturing throughput*. Report EPA-600/5-78-009 (Cincinnati, OH: US Environmental Protection Agency, 1978).

64 http://en.wikipedia.org/wiki/Efficient_energy_use (accessed July 23, 2012).

65 www.rmi.org/search-category/Energy+and+Resources/Energy+Efficiency/ sharepoint (accessed July 23, 2012).

66 McKinsey Global Institute, *Curbing Global Energy Demand Growth: The Energy Productivity Opportunity* (San Francisco, CA: McKinsey, 2007).

67 Sharma and Vredenburg, "Proactive Environmental Responsiveness Strategy."

68 www.apple.com/environment/ (accessed July 23, 2012).

69 www.pg.com/en_US/sustainability/environmental_sustainability/products_ packaging/index.shtml (accessed July 23, 2012).

70 A. Agarwal and P. Strachan, "Is Industrial Symbiosis only a Concept for Developed Countries?" *The Journal for Waste & Resource Management Professionals* (2008): 42.

71 www.indigodev.com/Kal.html (accessed November 7, 2012).

72 www.epa.gov/superfund/policy/cercla.htm (accessed June 15, 2012).

73 J.R. Copeland, Y. Feyman and M. O'Keefe, "A Report on Corporate Governance and Shareholder Activism," *Proxy Monitor Fall 2012 Report*, The Manhattan Institute for Legal Policy, www.proxymonitor .org/forms/pmr_04.aspx (accessed September 18, 2013).

74 S.L. Hart and S. Sharma, "Engaging Fringe Stakeholders for Competitive Imagination," *Academy of Management Executive* 18(1) (2004): 7-18.

75 M. Brophy and R. Starkey, "Environmental Reporting," in R. Welford (ed.), *Corporate Environmental Management 1, Systems and Strategies* (London: Earthscan, 1998).

76 http://en.wikipedia.org/wiki/Ken_Saro-Wiwa (accessed July 23, 2012).

77 A detailed description is provided in the case Brent Spar (A) & (B). IMD/Babson College. European case Clearing House.

78 www.interbrand.com/en/best-global-brands/best-global-brands-2008/ best-global-brands-2011.aspx (accessed July 23, 2012).

79 "When the Jobs Inspector Calls," *The Economist* (March 31, 2012): 73-6.

80 "Walmart's Mexican Morass," *The Economist* (April 28, 2012): 71-2.

81 S.J. Kobrin, "Oil and Politics: Talisman Energy and Sudan," *International Law and Politics*, 36 (2004): 425-56.

82 A. Hoffman, *SC Johnson and the Greenlist backlash*. Globallens Case Study (University of Michigan, 2013).

83 G. Topham, "Airline Industry: EU Emissions Trading Scheme 'Could Risk Trade War'," *The Guardian UK* (June 11, 2012).

84 "Airline Industry Favors Global Carbon Offsets," *Environment and Energy Management News* (May 14, 2013), www.environmental leader.com/2013/05/14/airline-industry-favors-global-carbon-offsets/ (accessed September 18, 2013).

85 Sharma and Vredenburg, "Proactive Environmental Responsiveness Strategy."

86 Hart and Sharma, "Engaging Fringe Stakeholders for Competitive Imagination."

Chapter 4

87 Emerging from its usage by the military since the 1990s, "VUCA" is a term that is often used to describe a high degree of turbulence and change in the environment. VUCA refers to volatility, uncertainty, complexity, and ambiguity in the environment.

88 P. Hawken, *The Ecology of Commerce: A Declaration of Sustainability* (New York: Harper Business, 1993).

89 J. Bosman, "After 244 Years, Encyclopaedia Britannica Stops the Presses," *New York Times* (March 13, 2012), http://mediadecoder .blogs.nytimes.com/2012/03/13/after-244-years-encyclopaedia-britannica-stops-the-presses/ (accessed April 10, 2014).

90 http://en.wikipedia.org/wiki/Negawatt_power.

91 L. Cohn, "Negawatts bats megawatts in New England," Realenergy-writers.com (2008), www.realenergywriters.com/ee-blog/2008/03/06/negawatts-beat-megawatts-in-new-england/ (accessed September 6, 2012).

92 *Ibid.*

93 www.interfaceglobal.com/Sustainability/Interface-Story.aspx (accessed September 6, 2012); www.interfaceglobal.com/ (accessed September 6, 2012).

94 *Ibid.*

95 J.T. Mayberry, "Growth Through Innovation: The Selective Pursuit of Opportunity," lecture delivered at the Schulich School-James Gillies Lecture, Toronto Eaton Centre Marriott (March 1, 2001).

96 Foundry-Planet.Com, "ArcelorMittal unveils new ultra low carbon steel technology at Dofasco plant," (October 8, 2010), www.foundry-planet.com/index.php?id=110&L=4&tx_ttnews[year]=2010&tx_ttnews[month]=08&tx_ttnews[day]=10&tx_ttnews[tt_news]=8774&cHash= 1b888e52e6cc6746f82998c77bf1954a (accessed October 1, 2013).

 97 Clayton M. Christensen, *The Innovator's Dilemma: The Revolutionary Book That Will Change the Way You Do Business* (New York: Harper Business, 2000).
 98 S.L. Hart and M. Milstein, "Creating Sustainable Value," *Academy of Management Executive* 17(2) (2003): 56-69.
 99 C.K. Prahalad and S. Hart, "The Fortune at the Bottom of the Pyramid," *Strategy+Business* 26 (2002): 54-67.
100 Hart and Milstein, "Creating Sustainable Value."

Chapter 5

101 These two patterns of decision-making were identified by Kahneman and Tversky who developed prospect theory. They explained the heuristics and biases that influence how individuals and managers make decisions. They conducted multiple experiments in different contexts and found these two dominant patterns of decision-making by managers within organizations. In 2002, Daniel Kahneman received the Nobel Prize in Economic Sciences for the joint work that he did with Amos Tversky (who died in 1996), on judgment and decision-making. The core of their research was published in two articles in *Science* (1974) and *American Psychologist* (1984).
102 *Ibid.*
103 D. Kahneman, *Thinking Fast and Slow* (New York: Farrar, Strauss & Giroux, 2011).
104 M.C. Maletz and N. Nohria, "Managing in the White Space," *Harvard Business Review* 79(2) (2001).
105 E.L. Thorndike, "A Constant Error in Psychological Ratings," *Journal of Applied Psychology* 4(1) (1920): 25-9.
106 A. Tversky and D. Kahneman, "Judgment under Uncertainty: Heuristics and Biases," *Science* 185 (1974): 1124, 1128-30.
107 S. Sharma, "Managerial Interpretations and Organizational Context as Predictors of Firm Choice of Environmental Strategies," *Academy of Management Journal* 43(4) (2000): 681-97; S. Sharma, A. Pablo and H. Vredenburg, "Corporate Environmental Responsiveness Strategies: The Role of Issue Interpretation and Organizational Context," *Journal of Applied Behavioral Science* 35(1) (1999): 87-109.
108 *Ibid.*
109 *Ibid.*

110 Hal Arkes and Catherine Blumer, "The Psychology of Sunk Cost," *Organizational Behavior and Human Decision Process* 35 (1985): 124-40.

111 Sharma, "Managerial Interpretations and Organizational Context as Predictors."

112 Sharma, "Managerial Interpretations and Organizational Context as Predictors;" Sharma, Pablo and Vredenburg, "Corporate Environmental Responsiveness Strategies."

113 K.E. Weick, "Enacted Sensemaking in Crisis Situations," *Journal of Management Studies* 24 (1988): 305-17.

114 www.patagonia.com/us/patagonia.go?assetid=2047 (accessed October 2, 2012).

115 www.thebodyshop-usa.com (accessed October 2, 2012).

116 J. Confino, "Interview: Unilever's Paul Polman on Diversity, Purpose and Profits," *The Guardian* (October 2, 2013), www.theguardian.com/sustainable-business/unilver-ceo-paul-polman-purpose-profits (accessed November 8, 2013).

117 www2.dupont.com/corp/en-us/our-company/vision.html (accessed October 1, 2012); http://origin.dupont.com/Our_Company/en_CA/glance/vision/index.html (accessed October 1, 2012).

118 Narrated by Paul Tebo during a presentation at a conference.

119 www.bcorporation.net/community/ben-jerrys (accessed October 2, 2013).

120 www.benjerry.com/activism/mission-statement (accessed October 3, 2012).

121 www.tata.com/company/articles/inside.aspx?artid=m73PWlDIJmU= (accessed October 3, 2012).

122 Sharma, "Managerial Interpretations and Organizational Context as Predictors."

123 F. Pearce, "Unilever Plans to Double its Turnover While Halving its Environmental Impact," *The Telegraph* (July 23, 2013), www.telegraph.co.uk/earth/environment/10188164/Unilever-plans-to-double-its-turnover-while-halving-its-environmental-impact.html (accessed November 8, 2013).

124 www.greenatworkmag.com/gwsubaccess/02julaug/cover04.html (accessed October 3, 2012).

125 C. Holliday, "Sustainable Growth the DuPont Way," *Harvard Business Review* (September 2001): 129-34.

126 *Siemens Sustainability Report 2008* (Berlin and Munich: Siemens AG, 2009), www.siemens.com.

127 *Ibid.*

128 D.C. Hambrick and S. Finkelstein, "Managerial Discretion: A Bridge between the Polar Views of Organizational Outcomes," in B.M. Staw and L.L. Cummings (eds.), *Research in Organizational Behavior* 4 (Greenwich, CT: JAI Press, 1987): 369-406.
129 This quote is from page 31 of L.J. Bourgeois III, "On the Measurement of Organizational Slack," *Academy of Management Review* 6 (1981): 29-39.
130 M.P. Sharfman, G. Wolf, R.B. Chase and D.A. Tansik, "Antecedents of Organizational Slack," *Academy of Management Review* 13(4) (1988): 601-14.
131 K. Goetz, "How 3M Gave Everyone Days Off and Created an Innovation Dynamo," *Co-design* (2011), www.fastcodesign.com/1663137/how-3m-gave-everyone-days-off-and-created-an-innovation-dynamo (accessed October 3, 2012).
132 3M, *A Century of Innovation: The 3M Story* (The 3M Company, 2002).

Chapter 6

133 S.L. Hart, "A Natural-Resource Based View of the Firm," *Academy of Management Review* 20(4) (1995): 986-1014; S. Winter, "Knowledge and Competence as Strategic Assets," in D. Teece (ed.), *The Competitive Challenge* (Cambridge, MA: Ballinger, 1987): 159-84.
134 J.B. Barney, "Firm Resources and Sustained Competitive Advantage," *Journal of Management* 17(1) (1991): 99-120.
135 M. Polanyi, *Personal Knowledge: Towards a Post-Critical Philosophy* (Chicago, IL: University of Chicago Press, 1962).
136 R. Reed and R.J. DeFillippi, "Causal Ambiguity, Barriers to Imitation and Sustainable Competitive Advantage," *Academy of Management Review* 15 (1990): 88-102.
137 *Ibid.*
138 Barney, "Firm Resources and Sustained Competitive Advantage."
139 R.E. Freeman, *Strategic Management: A Stakeholder Approach* (Marshfield, MA: Pitman Publishing, 1984).
140 S.L. Hart and S. Sharma, "Engaging Fringe Stakeholders for Competitive Imagination," *Academy of Management Executive* 18(1) (2004): 7-18.
141 R.J. Boland and R.V. Tenkasi, "Perspective Making and Perspective Taking in Communities of Knowing," *Organization Science* 6 (1995): 350-72.

142 Hart and Sharma, "Engaging Fringe Stakeholders for Competitive Imagination."

143 This quote is from page 245 of J. Nahapiet and S. Ghoshal, "Social Capital, Intellectual Capital, and the Organizational Advantage," *Academy of Management Review* 23 (1998): 242-66.

144 S. Sharma and H. Vredenburg, "Proactive Environmental Responsiveness Strategy and the Development of Competitively Valuable Organizational Capabilities," *Strategic Management Journal* 19(8) (1998): 729-53.

145 Hart and Sharma, "Engaging Fringe Stakeholders for Competitive Imagination."

146 J.G. March, "Exploration and Exploitation in Organizational Learning. *Organization Science* 2(1) (1991): 71-87.

147 P. May, A. Dabbs, P. Fernández-Dávila, V. da Vinha and N. Zaidenweber, *Corporate Roles and Rewards in Promoting Sustainable Development: Lessons Learned from Camisea* (Energy and Resources Group, University of California-Berkeley, May 1999).

148 C.K. Prahalad and S. Hart, "The Fortune at the Bottom of the Pyramid," *Strategy+Business* 26 (2002): 54-67.

149 The quote is from page 15 of I. Nonaka, "A Dynamic Theory of Organizational Knowledge Creation," *Organization Science* 5 (1994): 14-37.

150 *Ibid.*

151 C. Argyris, *Reasoning, Learning, and Action: Individual and Organizational* (San Francisco, CA: Jossey-Bass, 1982).

152 J.D. Westphal and L.P. Milton, "How Experience and Network Ties Affect the Influence of Demographic Minorities on Corporate Boards," *Administrative Science Quarterly* 45 (2000): 366-98.

153 Hart and Sharma, "Engaging Fringe Stakeholders for Competitive Imagination."

154 C. Argyris and D. Schon, *Organizational Learning: A Theory of Action Perspective* (Reading MA: Addison-Wesley, 1978).

155 Joseph A. Schumpeter, *Capitalism, Socialism and Democracy* (London: Routledge, 1994[1942]).

156 Hart, "A Natural-Resource Based View of the Firm."

157 Hart and Sharma, "Engaging Fringe Stakeholders for Competitive Imagination."

158 H. Itami, *Mobilizing Invisible Assets*, 2nd ed. (Cambridge, MA: Harvard University Press, 1987).

159 U. Wassmer, R. Paquin and S. Sharma, "The Engagement of Firms in Environmental Collaborations: Existing Contributions and Future Directions," *Business & Society,* published online (March 28, 2012).

160 A. Crane, "Exploring Green Alliances," *Journal of Marketing Management*, 14 (1998): 559-79; S. Vachon and R.D. Klassen, "Green Project Partnership in the Supply Chain: The Case of the Package Printing Industry," *Journal of Cleaner Production* 14 (2006): 661-71.

161 M. Daily, "Dow, GM Launch Largest Commercial Fuel Cell," *Reuters News* (February 10, 2004).

162 "McDonald's: The First Corporate Partnership," Environmental Defense Fund, http://www.edf.org/partnerships/mcdonalds (accessed October 9, 2013).

163 *Ibid.*

164 *Ibid.*

165 *Ibid.*

166 Schumpeter, "The Butterfly Effect," *The Economist* (November 2, 2013): 74.

167 F. von Malmborg, "Conditions for Regional Public–Private Partnerships for Sustainable Development—Swedish Perspectives," *European Environment* 13 (2003): 133-49.

168 Wassmer, Paquin and Sharma, "The Engagement of Firms in Environmental Collaborations."

169 www.dailycal.org. Archives (University of California at Berkeley, accessed October 9, 2013).

170 E.R. Stafford, M.J. Polonsky and C.L. Hartman, "Environmental NGO–Business Collaboration and Strategic Bridging: A Case Analysis of the Greenpeace–Foron Alliance," *Business Strategy and the Environment* 9 (2000): 122-35.

Chapter 7

171 C.K. Prahalad and S. Hart, "The Fortune at the Bottom of the Pyramid," *Strategy+Business* 26 (2002): 54-67.

172 S.L. Hart and T. London, "Developing Native Capability: What Multinational Corporations can Learn from the Base of the Pyramid," *Stanford Social Innovation Review* 3(2) (2005): 28-33.

173 C.K. Prahalad and A. Hammond, "Serving the World's Poor, Profitably—The Payoff for Investing in Poor Countries," *Harvard Business Review* (September 2002): 4-11.

174 E. Simanis, "Reality Check at the Bottom of the Pyramid," *Harvard Business Review* (June 2012): 120-5.

175 *Ibid.*

176 A. Karnani, "The Mirage of Marketing to the Bottom of the Pyramid," *California Management Review* 49(4) (2007): 90-111.

177 Hart and London, "Developing Native Capability."

178 www.bop-protocol.org/.

179 S.L. Hart and S. Sharma, "Engaging Fringe Stakeholders for Competitive Imagination," *Academy of Management Executive* 18(1) (2004): 7-18.

180 *Ibid.*

181 The term "base of the pyramid" began to acquire currency in the early 2000s to represent the foundation of the pyramid rather than the pejorative "bottom of the heap."

182 S. Sharma, H. Vredenburg and F. Westley, "Strategic Bridging: A Role for the Multinational Corporation in Third World Development," *Journal of Applied Behavioral Science* 30(4) (1994): 458-76.

183 R.E. Freeman, *Strategic Management: A Stakeholder Approach* (Boston, MA: Pitman, 1984).

184 R.K. Mitchell, B.R. Agle and D.J. Wood, "Toward a Theory of Stakeholder Identification and Salience: Defining the Principle of Who and What Really Counts," *Academy of Management Review* 22(4) (1997): 853-86.

185 www.kupnet.org/news/ (accessed November 11, 2013).

186 For a detailed description, see D. Dunn and K. Yamashita, "Microcapitalism and the Megacorporation," *Harvard Business Review* (August 2003): 46-54.

187 www.hpl.hp.com/india/research/documentauthensystem.html (accessed October 16, 2013).

188 M. Warner, "U. of Michigan Becomes 10th College to Join Boycott of Coke," *The New York Times* (December 31, 2005).

189 Schumpeter, "The Butterfly Effect," *The Economist* (November 2, 2013): 74.

190 For examples of each of these, see D. Collins, "Serving the Homeless and Low-Income Communities Through Business & Society/Business Ethics Class Projects: The University of Wisconsin-Madison Plan," *Journal of Business Ethics* 15(1) (1996): 67-85; Prahalad and Hart, "The Fortune at the Bottom of the Pyramid;" M. Starik, "Should Trees Have Managerial Standing? Toward Stakeholder Status for Non-human Nature," *Journal of Business Ethics* 14(3) (1995): 207-17.

191 Hart and Sharma, "Engaging Fringe Stakeholders for Competitive Imagination."

192 The description is from E. Simanis and S. Hart, *The Monsanto Company: Quest for Sustainability* (Washington, DC: World Resources Institute, 2000).

193 D.L. Spar and L.T. La Mure, "The Power of Activism: Assessing the Impact of NGOs on Global Business," *California Management Review* 45(3) (2003): 78-101.

194 For an in-depth discussion of this concept, see R. Chambers, *Rural Development: Putting the Last First* (London: Longman, 1984).

195 Mitchell, Agle and Wood, "Toward a Theory of Stakeholder Identification and Salience."

196 See B. Ellison, D. Moller and M.A. Rodriguez, *Hindustan Lever Reinvents the Wheel* (Barcelona: IESE, 2002).

197 www.hul.co.in/sustainable-living/casestudies/Casecategory/Project-Shakti.aspx (accessed October 22, 2013).

198 *Ibid.*

199 See H. McDonald, T. London and S. Hart, *Expanding the Playing Field: Nike's World Shoe Project* (Washington, DC: World Resources Institute, 2002).

200 See K. Herbst, "Enabling the Poor to Build Housing: Pursuing Profit and Social Development Together," *Changemakers.net Journal* (September 2002).

201 www.cemex.com/SustainableDevelopment/HighImpactSocialPrograms.aspx (accessed October 23, 2013).

202 J. Immelt, V. Govindarajan and C. Trimble, "How GE is Disrupting Itself," *Harvard Business Review* (October 2009): 3-11.

203 Sharma, Vredenburg and Westley, "Strategic Bridging: A Role for the Multinational Corporation."

204 *Ibid.*

205 L.D. Brown, "Bridging Organizations and Sustainable Development," *Human Relations* 44 (1991): 807-31; F. Westley and H. Vredenburg, "Strategic Bridging: The Collaboration Between Environmentalists and Business in the Marketing of Green Products," *Journal of Applied Behavioral Science* 27 (1991): 65-91.

206 Sharma, Vredenburg and Westley, "Strategic Bridging: A Role for the Multinational Corporation;" Westley and Vredenburg, "Strategic Bridging: The Collaboration Between Environmentalists and Business."

207 Sharma, Vredenburg and Westley, "Strategic Bridging A Role for the Multinational Corporation."

208 *Ibid.*

Chapter 8

209 H. Miller, "Australian Carbon Trading Scheme Commences: All Emissions Are Not Local," *Triple Pundit* (October 10, 2012), www .triplepundit.com/2012/10/australian-carbon-trading/ (accessed December 8, 2012).

210 A. Fiola, "European Carbon Market in Trouble," *The Washington Post* (May 5, 2013), http://articles.washingtonpost.com/2013-05-05/world/39048051_1_carbon-footprints-carbon-emissions-climate-change (accessed November 13, 2013).

211 B. Walsh, "As the World Keeps Getting Warmer, California Begins to Cap Carbon," *Time Science and Space* (December 4, 2012), http://science.time.com/2012/12/04/as-the-world-keeps-getting-warmer-california-begins-to-cap-carbon/ (accessed December 8, 2012).

212 P. Behr, "GE's Immelt Says US Policy Deadlock Holds Back Clean Energy Development," *Climatewire* (September 24, 2010), www.nytimes.com/cwire/2010/09/24/24climatewire-ges-immelt-says-us-policy-deadlock-holds-bac-86164.html (accessed April 12, 2014).

213 M. Starik and G.P. Rands, "Weaving an Integrated Web: Multilevel and Multisystem Perspectives of Ecologically Sustainable Organizations," *Academy of Management Review* 20(4) (1995): 908-35.

214 *Ibid.*

Index